EDUCATION, SOCIAL R ...ND
PHILOSOPHICAL DEVELOPMENT

Reflecting on the meaning and purpose of an education at the mercy of political changes and innovation, this book considers the social, historical, religious and cultural contexts that define education systems. With a particular focus on how historical contexts shape the nature of education and its relevance to wider society, it explores the history of education in relation to social reform, economic relevance and raising standards.

The first part of the book describes the developing system of education within England and Wales from the 19th century, with reference to the growing consciousness of the need for 'education for all'. The second part identifies key philosophical influences on the evolving understandings of education, and thereby of the developing policies and arrangements made in the light of those understandings which they generated. Finally, the third part of the book revisits the 'aims of education' in the light of the historical development and the philosophical critiques.

This book will be of great interest to academics, researchers, postgraduate students and policy makers interested in the history of education and the moments that have defined it.

Richard Pring is Emeritus Professor of Education, and was formerly Director of Department of Educational Studies, University of Oxford, UK.

EDUCATION, SOCIAL REFORM AND PHILOSOPHICAL DEVELOPMENT

Evidence from the Past, Principles for the Future

Richard Pring

 Routledge
Taylor & Francis Group

LONDON AND NEW YORK

First published 2022
by Routledge
2 Park Square, Milton Park, Abingdon, Oxon OX14 4RN

and by Routledge
605 Third Avenue, New York, NY 10158

Routledge is an imprint of the Taylor & Francis Group, an informa business

© 2022 Richard Pring

The right of Richard Pring to be identified as author of this work has been asserted by him in accordance with sections 77 and 78 of the Copyright, Designs and Patents Act 1988.

British Library Cataloguing-in-Publication Data
A catalogue record for this book is available from the British Library

Library of Congress Cataloging-in-Publication Data
Names: Pring, Richard, author.
Title: Education, social reform and philosophical development : evidence
  from the past, principles for the future / RIchard Pring.
Description: Abingdon, Oxon ; New York, NY : Routledge, 2021. | Includes
  bibliographical references and index.
Identifiers: LCCN 2021002927 (print) | LCCN 2021002928 (ebook) | ISBN
  9780367675424 (hardback) | ISBN 9780367675431 (paperback) | ISBN
  9781003131731 (ebook)
Subjects: LCSH: Education--Social aspects. | Education--Aims and
  objectives. | Education--Philosophy. | Education--Great
  Britain--History.
Classification: LCC LC191 .P754 2021 (print) | LCC LC191 (ebook) | DDC
  370.15--dc23
LC record available at https://lccn.loc.gov/2021002927
LC ebook record available at https://lccn.loc.gov/2021002928

ISBN: 978-0-367-67542-4 (hbk)
ISBN: 978-0-367-67543-1 (pbk)
ISBN: 978-1-003-13173-1 (ebk)

Typeset in Bembo
by SPi Global, India

CONTENTS

SUMMARY OF CHAPTERS

Part I: Historical evolution of education – its meaning and its provision

Chapter 1: Developing pattern and meaning of education from early 19th century

Chapter 1 looks at the developing pattern of education for England and Wales from the early 19th century, namely, (i) development from 'optional Elementary Education for the working class' to 'education for all' by 1870, (ii) reforms of Endowed Grammar and Public Schools, (iii) reforms of the Ancient Universities of Oxford and Cambridge. These reflected changing social and economic conditions, generating greater social consciousness and demanding better education for all. Justifications for reforms were analysed by four Royal Commissions, which however took for granted social class divisions as determinants of appropriate education. Subsequently, technical and vocational education were introduced due to the changing industrial scene. To meet these developments reform was needed of the national system and thus the creation of School Boards in the 1870 Education Act. But there remained agitation from the working class for a broader sense of education, partly resulting from the reformed franchise. Assumptions about what counts as 'education' began to be challenged under a broader conception of what is meant by human flourishing.

Chapter 2: Apprenticeships and practical learning

Chapter 2 reminds us of the system of apprenticeships in the overall development of education and training. Such practical learning is too often neglected in appreciation of the developing tradition of education – a neglect which in different ways affects policy and practice. On the other hand, with the developing new industries, old apprenticeships diminished; new kinds were required, for instance in plumbing and electrical skills. 'Professional apprenticeships' developed, and so did technical schools and colleges. However, although development of apprenticeships is historically significant, their importance lies especially in our appreciation and understanding of practical knowledge and learning and of the educational and aesthetic values which they embody, as witness the perennial value of the work by Ruskin and Morris.

Chapter 3: Primary and secondary education for all

The chapter continues with the further development of the educational system leading to the 1944 Education Act – the gradual transition from the Elementary Schools to Secondary Education for All, reflecting changing social attitudes and economic structures, and accompanied by changing ideas of what it means to be educated, as, for instance, in schools embracing preparation for citizenship in an expanded franchise and in the relevance of practical and cultural inheritance for everyone.

Chapter 4: Further Education and Youth Service

Earlier chapters made frequent reference to the growth of technical training in response to changing economic demands, and thus to the development of institutions dedicated to such training, often linked to industry. This chapter (concluding with reference to 'youth work') focuses on the rapid development of this more practical, vocational and usually part-time education and training, even providing ladders of opportunity to degree level, and enriching what is meant by 'education' within the changed economic and social circumstances.

Chapter 5: Shifting sands of qualifications

Significant determinants of the changing understanding of 'education', and thus of the curriculum in schools and colleges, are the qualifications which (i) define standards to be aimed at and skills and intellectual qualities to be attained, (ii) supposedly meet the economic needs which schools and colleges are asked to serve, (iii) differentiate between pupils according to perceived abilities and destinies. This chapter traces developments in school qualifications over the past 80 years, reflecting changing and disputed understandings of 'educational achievement' – in particular connections (or disconnections) between academic attainment and vocational relevance.

Chapter 6: Higher Education: its changing nature

Universities are not immune from radical changes in their seen relevance to society and the economy. Not only in their massive expansion to a much wider range of students, but also in the areas of intellectual concern, many of them have come to look as though belonging to different species from when Newman wrote *The Idea of a New University*. This is reflected partly in the changing conception of what counts as an 'educated person', partly in the control of standards intrinsic to that conception. The changes in what counts as University is traced in this chapter, raising questions about the aims and meaning of Higher Education.

Chapter 7: Religious influence: education and Faith Schools

Clearly the religious dimension cannot be omitted from our understanding both of the evolution of educational provision from early years to higher education and of how, within such provision, the very concept of what it means to be educated changes. This is particularly the case following the social change to a more secular society.

Chapter 8: Changing political control

From the end of the 19th century to the present, we have seen gradual change in control of schools, first, to School Boards in 1870, thence to Local Education Authorities in 1902, now (if they so choose) to self-standing Academy status or Multi-Academy Trusts (MATs) which, despite their proclaimed independence, relate directly to Central Government. At the same time, there has been a shift in control of curriculum from teachers to Government through legislation and national quali-fications. Increasing political control has entered, too, into Higher Education with the creation of the Office for Students (OfS). This chapter examines the complexity of these changes, the problems encountered in greater Government control, and the implications for education – both its provision and its characterisation.

Part II: Philosophical assumptions

Chapter 9: Summary of changing concept of 'education' with philosophical assumptions

The chapter draws on the historical development of 'education', as detailed in Part I, to pick out eight significant aspects affecting what it increasingly meant to be con-sidered 'educated', thereby affecting different institutional arrangements. It briefly summarises the changing ideas of 'being educated' and competing philosophical theories which underpinned these developments and which are examined critically in the succeeding three chapters.

Chapter 10: Utilitarianism, Idealism and Socialism

Chapters in Part I refer to the different philosophical influences presupposed in the changing policy, practice and indeed meaning of education, especially regarding dif-ferent social classes. Reference is made to the influence of Utilitarianism, but also, with regard particularly to the Public Schools and Universities, the Idealism (derived from the influence of Hegel) of such philosophers as T. H. Green and Samuel Coleridge. Such influence helped justify a hierarchy of schools for an enlightened ruling class or 'clerisy', but also stimulated a lasting influence on the aspiration for the 'cultivation of the intellect', reflected in Mathew Arnold's *Culture and Anarchy*. Idealism mitigated the dominance of Bentham's Utilitarianism but stimulated the onset of Socialist ideas, especially through the work of William Morris, John Ruskin and R. H. Tawney.

Chapter 11: Positivism, Post-Modernism, and wisdom of the market

There is danger of seeing different philosophical influences on the historically developing conception of education as mutually exclusive at any given time. But, on the contrary, we saw how, in the changing climate of the 19th century, both Utilitarianism and Idealism impinged on educational thinking, and how Socialist conceptions of society emerged partly from Idealist thinkers. What appear on the surface to be distinctive philosophies surprisingly, but jointly, interact in shaping political decisions and control over educational provision. Here we reflect on the influence of Positivism and the counter- influence of Post-Modernism (with the onset of 'Post-Truth'), but how this paradoxically encouraged contemporary iden-tification of educational aims to be associated with respect for the 'wisdom of the market'.

Chapter 12: Pragmatism

Pragmatism is a philosophical 'theory of meaning', closely associated with the 19th century American philosopher, C. S. Peirce, who focused on the central concept of 'belief' (not 'knowledge') and on the meaning of beliefs as being logically related to the actions which follow. A belief is acceptable only if it leads to successful actions and habits as predicted, but is open to correction if it fails to do so. John Dewey's theory and practice (taking the Pragmatist stance) were very influential in America, and in much educational thinking and practice in Britain, seeming to encourage 'activity-based' (rather than 'transmission of knowledge-based') curriculum – 'child-centred' rather than 'knowledge-centred'.

Chapter 13: Respect for truth: problems of political discourse

This chapter addresses the problems which have arisen from the need to reconcile differences emerging from disagreements over 'aims of education' and thus over relevant 'provision of education', against the background of different and often rival philosophical positions. Especially is this the case when the arguments bear the hall-marks of what is currently referred to as a 'post-truth society'.

Part III: Conclusion and way forward

Chapter 14: Aims of education: human flourishing and development of persons

This final chapter draws conclusions concerning the aims of education for all young people, emerging from, first, the historical account in Part I (which reflected social and economic changes) and, second, the competing philosophical assumptions given in Part II. It surely is a case (to return to Gary McCulloch statement in the Introduction) of it being very hard to understand education without recognising its historical characteristics … The interplay of past and present has special resonance when we are dealing with education. It offers us ample opportunity to make use of the wisdom of the past'.

INTRODUCTION

Historical understanding and philosophical reflection

Purpose of the book

Those familiar with the history of education in Britain would be aware of constant political changes and innovations, reflecting redefinitions of the 'meaning of education' and of the main purposes of 'educational provision' – so often reflecting the whims of incoming Secretaries of State. Throughout such changes, philosophers of education continue to redefine what is meant by 'education' as though achievable in isolation from broader historical contexts and philosophical assumptions in which those definitions are established. But is it not possible to attain a definition of education and its aims which would have universal application and, on the basis of which, one might look critically on the successive political and institutional changes and claims?

The book addresses that question in the changing historical context as one period succeeds another, each with its own assumptions about the nature of education and relevance to wider society under the banner of 'social reform', 'economic relevance' or 'raising standards'. In so saying, the book is motivated by Professor Gary McCulloch's 1993 Inaugural Lecture at Lancaster University (*Lessons from Class of 1944? History as Education*) in which he argues:

> It is very hard to understand education without recognising its historical characteristics ... The interplay past and present has special resonance when we are dealing with education. It offers us ample opportunity to make use of the wisdom of the past.
>
> (*reprinted in* Gordon, P., 1995, p. 250)

However, although prompted by the historical narratives, this book seeks further understanding of the conditions of those historical accounts, with this author's humble reference to the words of Michael Oakeshott (1975, p. vii) 'on human conduct'.

> Philosophical reflection is recognised here as the adventure of one who seeks to understand in other terms what he already understands and in which the understanding sought (itself unavoidably conditional) is a disclosure of the conditions of the understanding enjoyed and not a substitute for it.
>
> *(p.vii)*

Therefore, there is an intertwining of 'both understandings', especially in Part I, but a concentration on that further understanding provided by philosophical reflection in Part II.

Division of the book

Part I (Historical evolution of education) describes the developing system of education within England and Wales from the 19th century, with reference to the growing consciousness of the need for 'education for all', as educational provision responds to changing social conditions and economic demands, albeit rooted in different philosophical assumptions.

Part II (Philosophical assumptions) takes up the references necessarily made in Part I to underlying and conflicting philosophical justifications for changing educational practices. These assumptions and justifications are made more explicit, and examined critically.

Part III (Conclusion) revisits the 'aims of education' in the light of the historical development and the philosophical critiques.

The historical narrative relates particularly to England and Wales. In Scotland and Northern Ireland, 'education' comes under different administrations, but many of the issues, both historical and philosophical, are similar. Connections with the United States, both in organisational influence and in philosophical critique, especially in relation to John Dewey, are also made. After all, as one English Secretary of State once told this author, 'John Dewey was responsible for all the problems in our schools' – a charge repeated by a succeeding Minister of Education in the *Luna Caprese*, Oxford (now sadly closed down).

References

Gordon, P., 1995, McCulloch, G., 1993, Inaugural Lecture, 'Lessons from the class of 1944? History as Education', in Gordon, P., ed., *The Study of Education*, London: The Woburn Press.

Oakeshott, M., 1975, *On Human Conduct*, Preface, Oxford: Clarendon Press.

PART I

Historical evolution of education – its meaning and provision

The dominant views about education and its provision are by no means static – they have a history, reflecting the social and economic changes in the wider society, and therefore, as Professor McCulloch is quoted as saying in the Introduction,

> It is hard to understand education without recognising its historical characteristics.

One can see, therefore, in the following chapters, the ways in which the very concept of 'educated' reflected (especially at the beginning of our period) the social strata within society, but then the economic needs for a better-prepared workforce, the fight for greater recognition by the working class of their cultural needs, the increasing role of the arts and aesthetic appreciation, the quality of thinking of a newly enfranchised population.

One can also see the influence of competing philosophical views about the nature of knowledge, the common good, the ideals to be followed – all of which, having been raised in Part I, will be developed in much greater depth in Part II.

1

DEVELOPING PATTERN AND MEANING OF EDUCATION FROM EARLY 19TH CENTURY

Elementary beginnings

In 1833 the Government gave its first grant (£20,000) to subsidise Elementary Schools (though by no means covering all costs) in what would, four decades later, come to be a national system of schools available for all children. Already there were Elementary Schools, with religious foundations, run by the National Society for the Promotion of the Education of the Poor according to the Principles of the Established Church, and by the British and Foreign School Society of the Dissenters, which depended partly on small fees from working class and often impoverished families. But such schools were not everywhere and were often not in the very poor and deprived areas. Furthermore, the majority of attendants were boys, the girls being required for help with domestic responsibilities. It was not until the Forster Act of 1870 that there were established local School Boards with powers to raise rates to ensure Elementary Education for all, whether in Church Schools, already existing, or in the new Board Schools. A further Elementary Act of 1880 made such Elementary Education a legal requirement on all children aged 5–13, including girls, though often ignored in practice.

The provision of money by Government to support schools had its adversaries, namely, to some extent, religious bodies, who could be suspicious of State interference in what were religious provisions. As shall be seen in subsequent chapters, the relative authority of the Churches in protecting the role of religious understanding in the idea of the educated person would remain a permanent feature of the developing educational system.

There was, however, also political suspicion of State interference in public education. When a Member of Parliament enquired into an adequate system of national education, it was rejected because, amongst other things 'some Members were uneasy about this kind of state interference' in public education (as detailed by Lawton and Gordon, 1987, p.7).

None the less, it was finally agreed in 1839 that a Committee of the Privy Council be established to oversee the distribution of the grant, subject to supervision by a small inspectorate, which was the beginning of Her Majesty's Inspectorate, destined to play an important role in the development of the education system for 150 years. A key member of the Inspectorate from its early years was Matthew Arnold who held this position for thirty-five years (1851–1886) and whose thoughts about Elementary and Secondary Education had much influence on their formation (*as described in Chapter 2 and subsequently Chapter 10*).

By 1900, there were over 2,500 School Board Elementary Schools as well as 14,000 denominational Elementary Schools, mainly Church of England, but also Non-conformist, and now also Catholic as a result of their promotion after 1850 by Cardinal Wiseman, following the influx of immigrants due to the famine in Ireland.

However, arguments, arising from wider social concerns and pressures, had been leading Government, long before 1870, to provide a more comprehensive amount of grant to support the voluntary system of schools run by the National Schools Society and British and Foreign Schools Society. In 1839, for example, Kay-Shuttleworth, secretary of the Committee of Council, who (1832) had produced a book entitled *The Moral and Physical Conditions of the Working Class in Manchester*, became a strong advocate of educational provision for all working-class children.

> If they (the working classes) are to have knowledge, surely it is part of a wise and virtuous government to do all in its power to secure them useful knowledge and to guard them against pernicious opinions.

Indeed, the conditions in which so many of the working class lived were extremely poor and sorely needed to be addressed. As Matthew Arnold reported,

> He saw their filthy and ragged children daily in the schools, children eaten up with disease, half-sized, half-fed, half-clothed, neglected by their parents, without health, without home, without hope.
>
> (Arnold, M., 1869, Editorial, p. xxxv)

One argument increasingly influential was that improved working-class conditions, which should include education, would be necessary to avert social revolution. But organised working-class bodies, such as the London Working Men's Association (founded in 1836 and seeking political support for its 'People's Charter') and the Miners Association of Great Britain and Ireland, sought for schools to be financed from public funds, freed from religious teaching and administered by democratically elected local committees. By 1849, the original £20,000 annual grant, given to the National Society's and the British and Foreign Schools Society's Elementary Schools, had been raised to £125,000.

However, an undated pamphlet of the 1850s argued that

> In the midst of England's 'unparalleled wealth, luxury and power', those in authority have defrauded the labourers and reduced them to an animal existence. It is, then, the government's responsibility to set a tax on the property of the country to raise funds for a national system of secular education for the people.
>
> (*paraphrased by* Simon, 1960, p. 343)

Certainly, an ever-increasing number of organisations representing working-class men (for example, Mechanics Institute founded in 1824, Amalgamated Society of Engineers, London Working Men's Association for Promoting National Secular Education, and Miners' Association of Great Britain and Ireland) were calling for a National System of Education, which would apply to the working class. William Newton, who became the first independent Labour candidate for Parliament in 1852, expressed concern that keeping the people in a state of ignorance is made the ground of their exclusion from political power. No doubt the significance of those growing concerns led to the Franchise Act of 1867 which, unlike the Franchise Act of 1832, extended the franchise to include those from the skilled working class.

It is important to note, however, that the forces behind the urge to extend education through a National System were by no means arising only from the working-class's perceived benefits of such education or from middle-class wish for greater security. Deeper philosophical arguments were made by the likes of Jeremy Bentham and James Mill whose ethical principles called for 'the greatest amount of happiness of the greatest number', including the widest possible institution of property. As Simon (1960, p. 144) explained,

> the Utilitarians stood, in theory, for a rational, secular, scientific education for all, providing the enlightenment for achieving such happiness.
>
> (*Chapter 10 gives an extended account of the educational significance of Utilitarianism.*)

At the same time, there was the influence of a quite different philosophical tradition, namely, that of the *Idealists* such as Thomas Carlisle, Samuel Taylor Coleridge and T. H. Green, amongst others – a tradition and an influence which will, alongside that of *Utilitarianism*, be explained more fully in Chapter 10.

Shaping of national education through Royal commissions

(i) **Popular Education in England – Newcastle Commission (1858–1861)**
Given the evolving nature of Elementary Education (benefiting from increased Government support, actively demanded by working-class societies and movements,

and now joined by esteemed political philosophical thinkers), it seemed appropriate that there should be established a Royal Commission to

> enquire into the present state of Popular Education in England, and to consider and report what Measures, if any, are required for the Extension of sound and cheap elementary instruction to all classes of the People.

The Commission's Report estimated that 860,000 children attended private schools, and some 1,675, 000 were in schools run by voluntary bodies (mainly the churches). Many schools, however, in poor areas or in rural parishes were in receipt of no support from public funds. Very few pupils stayed in school beyond the age of 11. But, unlike former Commissions, the Newcastle Commission resulted in no specific recommendations or legislation for improving Elementary Schools education, unless one were to include the scheme of 'payment by results' introduced by Robert Lowe, then in charge of the Education Department, and in keeping with the purposes of the Commission as set out above.

According to Lowe's proposal, payment to schools would depend on the examinations set by the visiting inspectorate ('payment by results'). As he declared to Parliament (Simon, 1960, p.349),

> I cannot promise the House that this system will be an economical one, and I cannot promise that it will be an efficient one, but I can promise that it will be one or the other. If it is not cheap, it shall be efficient; if it is not efficient it shall be cheap.

It was, therefore, incorporated into the *Revised Code* of 1863. But otherwise the Voluntary Schools 'system', though with increase of funding dependent on 'payment by results', remained untouched.

The remaining years, however, leading up to the Great Reform Act of 1870 (which was to bring the much-desired radical changes to the educational system) saw the increasing struggle of the working class, through their unions and other organisations, to get proper recognition in their demand for universal suffrage – and most importantly for an educational system which would be a key element in such suffrage. As Lowe, finally but reluctantly, argued

> I believe it will be absolutely necessary to compel our future masters to learn their letters.

> (quoted in Simon, 1960, p.355)

Education was thus coming to be seen as a political necessity in the reforms which were emerging. In this, one can see the underlying influence of the liberal, ethical and utilitarian theorising of Bentham and James Mill, referred to earlier, in which, to serve the welfare of all mankind, those making the decisions and leading the arguments require that wider vision and means of understanding.

On the other hand, there remained the assumption, even in a reformed system, that there should be different types of education for different classes of people. Thus the reform of the Elementary School system called also for reform of the education of those of a higher class (to be pursued further by Clarendon and Taunton Commissions, as shown below). Thus, according to Lowe, if the lower classes are to be educated so as to be qualified for the power which has passed into their hands, then the higher classes require to be better educated in order to preserve their position by 'superior education and superior cultivation', and thereby assert their authority by their 'greater intelligence and leisure'. In so doing, they might

> conquer back by means of a wider and more enlightened cultivation some of the influence which they have lost by political change.
>
> (Lowe, R., 1867, 1, 8–10)

However, here, as the radical reforms of 1870 approached, there was also emerging a much more positive understanding of the education of the working class. F. D. Maurice, in his book *Representation and Education of the People*, articulated the beliefs of the London's Working Men's College (founded in the early 1850s), when he argued that no so-called education would be good for the workers

> which did not recognise them as English citizens and did not aim directly at the object of qualifying them to perform their duties as citizens.
>
> (Maurice, F.D., 1866)

Thus. 'citizenship' had now entered into the list of educational aims as a result of anticipated political reforms.

In 1869, following the second meeting of the newly formed Trades Union Congress, the different Unions founded the National Education League which strongly advocated free and compulsory education, paid for by local rates, and non-sectarian.

However, there were other influences, too. The Paris exhibition of 1867 revealed how more advanced other countries, especially Germany, were in technical training and in universal Elementary Education. This was seen to be a challenge to the developing industrialisation of Britain, as was made clear from W. E. Forster's enquiry among Chambers of Commerce in 1867–8 (see Simon, 1960, p. 360). Partly as a result of this adverse understanding of Britain's development in technical education, there was established a Royal Commission on Technical Instruction, which sat between 1881 and 1884.

To conclude this subsection, the story so far is the prelude to the 1870 Education Act, succeeded by the 1880 Elementary Education Act, which initiated a universal, free system and compulsory education for all young people aged 5 to 13. As such an ideal emerged, and in looking to the future, it is useful to reflect back on the evolving idea of education. Initially, 'to be educated' was seen to be relevant to a very limited class of people, namely, those who by reason of birth had the intelligence and the social position to engage in what were seen to be educational activities and to be prepared for social and political responsibilities. The concept of 'social class', therefore, was central to the understanding of education, that is, of what it meant to be 'an educated person'. As we shall see, such a conception remained much longer than the universal agreement on *Elementary Education* for all, and would be powerfully advocated in the almost contemporary Royal Commission, namely, the Clarendon Commission on Public Schools.

On the other hand, a connection had been made between 'education' and preparation for citizenship, a preparation seen to be increasingly important as universal franchise was conceded, even if at first the virtues of citizenship were initially to emphasise the importance of respecting and retaining class structure of society. But it was a limited view of 'duties as citizens' within the very class-based society and thus a limited understanding of 'education'.

Finally, the economic need for literacy, amongst the working class, was increasingly recognised, as technical ability and initiative were seen to be important in the changing and competitive industrial economy.

(ii) **Public Schools: Clarendon Commission** – *leading to Public Schools Act of 1868*

At the same time as the completion of the Newcastle Commission on Elementary Schools, there were further Royal Commissions, followed by Acts of Parliament, to reform both the Public Schools and the Endowed Grammar Schools in order

> to meet the needs of the Victorian upper middle class … . And to remodel the Endowed Grammar Schools on three grades to serve three different social levels or occupational groupings.
>
> (Simon, 1960, p. 11)

Thus, in1861 the Clarendon Commission was established to examine the nine major 'public schools' (namely, Eton, Harrow, Rugby, Winchester, Westminster, Charterhouse, St. Paul's, Merchant Taylors', Shrewsbury), though not including the two girls' Private Schools, namely. Cheltenham Ladies College, founded in 1853, and Roedean, founded in 1885. Why was there seen to be the need for reform in the light of public interest?

First, it was the view of the Chairman, the Earl of Clarendon, that reform was essential because their inefficiency placed

> the upper classes in a state of inferiority to the middle and lower'.
>
> (quoted in Simon, 1960, p. 304)

Once again, the changing economic and social context demanded places for an expanded social clientele, not just the socially exclusive landed gentry but also the 'upper middle class' serving the different economic context, as the industrial revolution developed and as the Endowed Grammar Schools themselves were reforming accordingly.

Second, the social elite attending such schools required a reformed education and curriculum. In such a context, the quality of education needed much improvement. For example, at Winchester

> the curriculum was almost exclusively classical … From about 1820 it was possible to learn French as an 'extra' out of school hours, and Mathematics from the writing master, a despised functionary whose main duty was to clean slates and mend the pens. There was, of course, no Science. All this rested upon the belief, typical of an aristocratic age, that in the Classics were to be found, perfectly expressed, all the principles and mental discipline required to train the statesman, the divine and the gentleman… Critical judgment, taste and facility were held to flow as a natural consequence from a thorough training in Greek and Latin.
>
> (Firth, 1949, p. 107)

Reforms were necessary. Greek and Latin were demanded by the more Radical middle class now emerging, especially after there was introduced competitive entry to the Civil Service and to colonial administration, and as there were increasing demands for educated personnel for the growing businesses of the mid-19th century. Thus were introduced gradually mathematics, sciences and modern languages, with less emphasis accordingly on Latin and Greek.

But, thirdly, such reforms needed to be treated with caution. In a letter to the Commissioners, Gladstone, an old Etonian (shortly to become leader of the Liberal Party and thence Prime Minister), advocated retention of Classics as 'the paramount matter of education' for the 'public good', which was required not only for business efficiency and modernisation of studies but also for

> the maintenance of aristocratic exclusiveness – of a form of education which was remarkably different from that available to other classes.
>
> (Simon, 1960)

Hence, Classics would be retained as 'the paramount matter of education' for that small proportion of youth destined for high office in public duties and in the wider economy and who were to 'become in the fullest sense educated men'. Such might be referred to as the 'clerisy' (Coleridge's word, as explained in Chapter 10) which would continue, despite reforms, to shape the educational system for the Public Schools, as argued in the *Report of the Public School Commission* (*Vol. I. 56*), which

> have had perhaps the largest share in moulding the character of an English gentleman.

The situation in the closing decades of the 19th century is summed up by Simon (1960, p. 318)

All in all, by insisting on the preservation of the classics as the main core of teaching, and by ensuring the final separation of the Public Schools from those for other classes, the Clarendon Commission created an efficient and entirely segregated system of education for the governing class – one that had no parallel in any other country.

Therefore, by way of conclusion, the 'reform' of the Public Schools had three key aspects.

First, it recognised the need to improve quality of the teaching as well as content. Schools could not ignore advances in science in the education of the next generation.

Second, there was perpetuated the view that those privileged to be in the top ranks of society needed those studies – found in the Classics – which formed them as 'gentlemen'. The classics would introduce them to a mental mind-set which was seen to prepare pupils for positions of responsibility in the society to which they were destined.

Third, such a mental mind-set would be inspired by Plato's *Republic*, which, far from advocating democracy as a form of government, strongly argued for maintenance of a 'Guardian Class' formed with the wisdom which comes from the right sort of education and upbringing. Such 'Guardians' would be recognised by the relevant virtues, especially those of justice and fairness which should characterise life in the State as a whole. Moral development would be at the centre of the education of the Guardian Class as they would be nurtured to perceive what constitutes a 'good life'.

(iii) Endowed Grammar and Proprietary Schools: Taunton Commission, 1868 *(leading to the Endowed Schools Act of 1889)*

In 1864, the Taunton Commission was appointed to examine the state of education for

> those large classes of English society which are comprised between the humblest and the very highest,

namely, those between Elementary Schools for the poor and working class, on the one hand, and, on the other, Public Schools dedicated to 'moulding the character of an English gentleman'. These were mainly the 'endowed schools' (over 800 of them), generally, though not exclusively, called Grammar Schools, and endowed to serve the public good, especially in an age when a better educated middle class was needed to serve the changing professional needs and the more industrial economy. But there were also private (not endowed) or Proprietary Schools included in the Taunton Commission enquiry.

However, the 'candidates' for such schools (to be considered by the Taunton commissioners) varied 'in social class terms' according to occupational groupings. Indeed, it was proposed by one commissioner, Lord Harrowby, that

> I should like to say, you shall be a good lower-class school; you shall be a middle middle-class school; and you shall be a higher middle-class school, that which is now called a Grammar School.
>
> (Report of the Schools Inquiry Commission, Vol. I, 577/8
> ref. Simon, 1960, p. 323)

Such different grades of school would have different mainly occupational purposes, with the top grade's purposes including the eventual possibility of entry to University.

However, in this evolving pattern of schooling, endowments previously supporting local Elementary Schools for the poor were transferred to support the new kinds of middle-class schools, thereby depriving the poorer people of the financial support for their children.

Each of the Royal Commissions, therefore, arose from perceived problems in the educational provisions of the country. They saw themselves, in their respective recommendations, to be rectifying weaknesses both in the provision of education and thereby in the very understanding of what it means to be educated – the two were not unrelated. There was clearly a view that provision of education and its purpose were, or should be, distinctive for those in the population 'between the humblest and the very highest'. The very concept of education was inseparable from the needs and abilities of the working class, on the one hand (dealt with by the Newcastle Commission), and, on the other hand, the upper class destined for leadership within society (dealt with by the Clarendon Commission). In between were those who attended Endowed Grammar Schools, many of whom, following the third Reform Act of 1884, would have gained the right to vote. and who needed to be sufficiently educated to undertake employment in the expanding industrial landscape or in certain professions. Altogether, following that Act, roughly one out of every eight persons would have gained the right to vote (according to Cole, 1941, p.6.), and needed to be sufficiently educated to undertake employment in the expanding industrial landscape or certain professions.

But the demands on those entering into the expanding industries and professions would be at different levels, thereby suggesting different educational requirements. Hence, just as there was a distinction to be made between the educational needs and abilities of 'the humblest' and those of 'the very highest', so too one was able with profit to distinguish between the educational needs within this large middle group of school children. In effect, therefore, following the Taunton Commission Report, three different levels of education were recommended between the 'humblest' and the 'highest', and the top one of those three retaining the title of 'Grammar School' – creating, in effect, further different classes within society each with a distinctive social role.

(iv) **Universities: Royal Commission 1850–1853**, *leading to Oxford Univ. Act of 1854, and Cambridge Univ. Act of 1856*

However, the new initiative of establishing Commissions, followed by reforming legislation, into the nation's educational institutions was not confined to the 'hierarchy of schools', whether Elementary, Grammar or Public, but also applied to the University system. There was growing concern both within the University of Oxford and in Parliament that the Universities (with special regard to Oxford) needed to embrace developments in science (too long ignored) as well as 'the principles also of sound and enlarged intellectual culture', as referred to in Appendix

A of the 1852 *Report of the Oxford University Commission* (see Simon, 1960, p.291). There was a change in the intellectual climate as reflected in Mark Pattison's *Memoirs of an Oxford Don* (1884/1988, p. 123).

> From that moment [1845] dates the regeneration of the University. Our thoughts reverted to their proper channel, that of the work we had to do ... We were startled when we came to reflect that the vast domain of physical science had been hitherto wholly excluded from our programme. The great discoveries of the last half century in chemistry, physiology, etc., were not even known by report to any of us.

But such 'regeneration' was felt by such leading figures as Jowett of Balliol College to require a jolt from outside the University to achieve the much-needed reforms. A Royal Commission was established to enquire into the Universities of Oxford, Cambridge and Dublin

> with a view to assist in the adaptation of those important institutions to the requirements of modern times.

Against considerable opposition from within the University (deriving from its cherished traditional independence), the Oxford University Bill was passed by Parliament in 1854 – the Cambridge Bill in 1856 – thereby making the Universities more relevant to the changing social and economic life and intellectual challenges of the country, including inevitably the reforms to the Endowed Grammar Schools – and yet retaining what the philosopher Coleridge referred to as 'the clerisy', an intellectual elite which, by reason of their education (essentially classical) was seen to have insight into what was good for society and its people.

Elementary education for all: 1870 Education Act

The slow evolution of educational thinking and policy throughout the 19th century came to a partial conclusion in the 1870 *Elementary Education Act*, often referred to as the Forster Education Act. According to this Act of Parliament, there was to be Elementary Education for all children, boys and girls, between the ages of 5 and 13 (though not necessarily compulsory until 1880, nor entirely free for everyone). This would be provided by either newly established Local School Boards or the Churches (Anglican, but also Non-Conformist and Catholic, as presently was the case). From 1870 to 1880, between 3000 and 4000 Elementary Schools were taken over by School Boards. Such a requirement was designed partly to prevent early employment of child labour.

However, assurance of overall provision (Church as well as non-Church schools) would be provided by these newly created Local School Boards, which were empowered eventually to make schooling compulsory within their respective areas. One major significance of this creation of local responsibility for educational provision was the shift in control of Elementary Schooling from Parliament (and thus from landed gentry) to nascent 'local authorities', on which the working class could gain representation as well as women, even though women did not have the franchise for electing members to Parliament until much later. Moreover, School Boards were empowered to raise funds from rates to help pay for the running of schools, to create more non-denominational schools where voluntary provision of the Churches was inadequate, to pay fees for the poorest children, and, if necessary, to create new by-laws making attendance compulsory between ages 5 and 13. The only religious education to be imposed would be the reading of the Bible.

On the other hand, such changes needed to be filtered through the perceptions of a rigidly hierarchical vision of society, where the highest level or class might enhance their social status as 'gentlemen' and as the 'guardian class' or 'clerisy' (to be explained in Chapter 10 concerned with underlying philosophical assumptions of these developments). At the lower end of the social spectrum, minimal education was being offered through the voluntary Elementary Schools provided by the Anglican, Non-conformist and later Catholic churches, now expanded considerably through the creation and rapid expansion of School Board Schools. Furthermore, that hierarchy was expanded *within* the Elementary system, as in some School Boards distinctions were made between Elementary Schools as such and Higher Grade Elementary Schools. Only gradually did all these receive funding from the rates.

Thereby was created a hierarchy of schools (followed by Universities for a limited few, mainly the product of Public Schools) which was perceived to be relevant both to the country's economic demands and to its social order: first, Public Schools; second, Endowed Grammar Schools; third, Elementary Schools (they being divided in many localities into Higher Grade Elementary Schools and the others). Higher Grade schools pointed the way to the eventual need for Secondary Schools for the continuing education of the more-able Elementary School children. The 1870 Act was thus leading to the 1902 Act.

In many respects, these developments, reflecting the struggles of increasingly organised working men who demanded basic education for their children as befits citizens and skilled workers, were showing success, although not yet progressing into Secondary Education.

There were, however, objections particularly on religious questions. The Non-conformists did not want their rate-payers' money to be supporting Church of England Elementary Schools. Nor did they want their children, if in School Board Schools, to be taught the doctrines of the Church of England. A compromise had to be found which would prevail for a hundred years, namely, the insertion of *Cowper-Temple Clause*, according to which School Board schools would have to be non-denominational in teaching religion, and also parents would have the legal right to have their children withdrawn from classes where religion was being taught. One shall see in Chapter 7 how this problem over different religious as well as secular loyalties was partly to be resolved through the establishment of Voluntary Controlled and Voluntary Aided schools, as well as non-religious State schools, although all would be within the State system but under the general supervision of the subsequent respective Local Education Authorities.

Development of technical education

Royal Commissions, as summarised above, had surprisingly little or nothing to say about the growing concern over the need for a different kind of post-Elementary School education to meet the needs of the rapid changes in the Industrial Society which was emerging in the latter half of the century. The centuries-old apprenticeship system (to be described in Chapter 2) was diminishing rapidly due to the Great Depression (which began in 1878, lasting twenty years) and to industrialisation which replaced the old trade skills with a much more mechanised system of production. Consequently, there were slowly emerging, especially in the London area at the beginning, 'Trade Schools'. 'Commercial Schools' and 'Junior Technical Schools' which focused on preparing for specific industries and their needs – the Technical Schools, particularly, on the growing needs of engineering industries. But by 1901 there were Technical Institutes (for example, according to Spens Report (1938), for furniture and cabinet making at the Shoreditch Technical Institute). This gradual growth of Technical Schools and Institutes, and indeed establishment of Technical Instruction Committees, arising from the decay of apprenticeships, sought to prepare entry to employment at the end of Elementary Schooling. Some of these were supported by local industrialists, and, as will be recounted in Chapter 6, eventually became integrated into the new Civic Universities.

Such was the growing significance of these developments in technical education that in 1873 the Royal Society of the Arts instituted examinations in the technological subjects and the City and Guilds of the London Institute did so in 1878. From 1881 to 1884 there was a further Royal Commission, namely, the Royal Commission on Technical Instruction. Finally, Members of Parliament formed the National Association for the Promotion of Technological and Secondary Education, providing a powerful lobby for improving the capacity of those who would be needed in the various national industries – yet another aspect of developments stimulated by unfavourable comparisons with other countries and resulting from performances at Paris and other international exhibitions. In 1889 there was the Technical Instructions Act informing such industrial training.

Interim conclusion: are there lessons to be learnt?

Changes to what was happening in educational provision, and in its underlying values, were rapid, as we have seen, due in part to the inauguration of Royal Commissions, which covered the provision of education from Elementary Schools to Universities, and reflecting:

- Changing economic needs of society;
- Necessary knowledge and skills required at all levels of the expanding economy (including science in Grammar Schools, technical education served by Technical Instruction Committees, Higher Grade Elementary Schools and Universities);
- Attempts to meet the requirements of both secular and religious bodies, reflecting different assumptions concerning the aims of education;

- Increasing demands of the working class for the education which would empower them as voting citizens;
- Nonetheless, a prevailing acceptance and importance of social class – especially the 'guardian class' formed through birth and privileged education.

Moreover, such changes needed to be filtered through the perceptions of a rigidly hierarchical vision of society, where the highest level or class might enhance their social status as 'gentlemen' and as the 'guardian class' (explained at greater length in Chapter 10, concerned with underlying philosophical assumptions of these developments). At the lower end of the social spectrum, minimal education was being offered initially through voluntary Elementary Schools provided by Anglican, Non-conformist and later Catholic Churches, but expanded considerably through creation of School Board Schools in 1870. Furthermore, that hierarchy was expanded within the Elementary system, with distinctions made between Elementary Schools as such and Higher Grade Elementary Schools. Only gradually did these receive funding from the rates.

The significance of such prevailing class attitudes upon the dilatory improvement of Elementary Education for the poor is illustrated well by the then Permanent Secretary of the Education Department.

> The staff of distinguished and aristocratic scholars from the universities treated Elementary Education and elementary teachers with contempt. Their cherished creed was that no education mattered or was of any real value except Classics and Mathematics … They had no use for … any idea that a child from the 'lower classes' might, after all, possess a modicum of brains. A ploughman's son was destined to be a ploughman as his father was.
>
> (Kekewich, 1920, p. 10)

On the other hand, towards the end of the century, it was shown how success in a competitive industrial market needed workers better trained in the technical know-how and skills of the different industries. This needed to be made possible at different levels and in different kinds of institution. Moreover, evolution of Higher Grade Schools pointed the way to the eventual need for Secondary Schools for the continuing education of the more-able Elementary School children. The 1870 Act was clearly leading to the 1902 Act!

None the less, there were voices, ever more powerful, in the future shaping of public opinion and political policy, concerning the nature of educational aims and educational provision, not confined to economic usefulness. Certainly workers, through different associations, were gradually uniting in demands for properly funded education for their children and themselves, to provide the literacy and numeracy skills needed for the more demanding and changing economy. However, that appeal for education went beyond the need for better literacy and numeracy. As Thomas Mann (an early socialist pioneer and a leader of the Miners' and Dockers' Strikes in the late 19th century) argued (see Simon, 1965, p. 40)

The demand we, as workmen, now make is for *leisure*, not idleness. Leisure to think, to learn, to acquire knowledge, to enjoy, to develop, in short, leisure to live,

and further

we claim more – we yearn for culture, we demand opportunities for physical and mental development, and we openly and fearlessly declare war against all that tends to keep us riveted to the earth.

Moreover, those demands increasingly focussed also on the knowledge required for intelligent participation as citizens, as the franchise gradually expanded to include the working class. As Simon (1965, p. 18) sums this up:

The new *Socialist* groups embarked on a programme of propaganda and education which brought a new conception of the potentialities of living and new hope to the more advanced sections of the working class [or, in the words of William Morris] a vision of a society in which labour would be pleasurable and education the right of all.

More controversially, an increasing voice in this working-class solidarity for education and citizenship was that of secular societies, represented through the Socialist Democratic Federation (SDF) of which Thomas Mann was a leading member, believing that the educational budget from the rates should not support particular religious beliefs and forms of life – a matter which affected provisions in the 1870 Act.

Finally, it had dawned that advance in educational provision and development required greater local responsibility in organisations than that provided by the thousands of School Boards, later to be legally created in Local Education Authorities in the Balfour Act of 1902.

References

Arnold, M. 1869, *Culture and Anarchy*, Cambridge University Press (1932 edition).

Cole, G.D.H., 1941, *British Working Class Politics, 1832–1914*, London: R.K.

Firth, J.D'E., 1949, *Winchester College*, London: Winchester Publications Ltd.

Kay-Shuttleworth, 1832, *The Moral and Physical Conditions of the Working Class in Manchester*, London: Ridgeway.

Kekewich, G.W., 1920, *The Education Department and After*, London: Constable.

Lawton, D. and Gordon, P., 1987, *HMI*, London: Routledge and Kegan Paul.

Lowe, R., 1867, *Primary and Classical Education*, Edinburgh: Edmonston and Douglas.

Maurice, F.D., 1866, *Representation and Education of the People*.

Morris, W., 1884, *On Art and Socialism* (ed. Holbrook Jackson, 1947).

Pattison, M., 1884/1988, *Memoirs of an Oxford Don*, London: Cassell.

Simon, B., 1960, *Studies in the History of Education, 1780–1902*, London: Lawrence and Wishart.

Simon, B., 1965, *Education and the Labour Movement, 1870–1920*, London: Lawrence and Wishart.

Spens Report, 1938, *Secondary Education with Special Reference to Grammar Schools and Technical High Schools*, London: HMSO.

2

APPRENTICESHIPS AND PRACTICAL LEARNING

Lessons to be learnt

Introduction

The editor's Introduction to the 1932 edition of Arnold's *Culture and Anarchy* states that

> there is indeed another kind of culture than that derived from 'the best that has been known and thought in the world. ... . It is the culture that springs from the common life of the people, the culture which means cultivation of the ordinary soul of the human spirit, which sanctifies the work that men do with their hands and makes significant and beautiful the labour wherewith they earn their bread.
>
> (1869/1932, p. xxxv)

In the work of William Morris, a disciple of Arnold, there was conceivably a different kind of education (reflected in his paper, 1881, 'On Art and Socialism') closely tied to the occupations of the working class, although such education is even today unfortunately often contrasted with 'education' by being called simply 'vocational training'.

It is important for the purposes of this book to be reminded of this culture and its embodiment in the long and ancient tradition of apprenticeships, especially in the light of William Morris' account of the aesthetic dimension and of the nature of 'practical knowledge', which are explained towards the end of this chapter and which are too often neglected in the promotion of personal development – a neglect which affects (or should affect) profoundly the provision of education in schools, colleges and higher education.

Apprenticeships: a long tradition

The practice and the idea of 'apprenticeship' have a long history. However, like all educational practices and ideas with long histories, they change over time, due (in the case we are considering) to changing economic forces as well also to political expediency.

A summary of the early beginning would refer to the Guilds established in the Middle Ages, the earliest mentioned being in 1156. These were associations of craftsmen focusing on a particular trade, who would be indentured such that there were reciprocal obligations between 'master" and 'apprentice'. The Master Craftsman would personally teach the young apprentice, take responsibility for his welfare (moral and material), and provide board and lodgings. The apprentice would be indentured for seven years before presenting his *chef d'oeuvre*. Following such success, he could continue as a *journeyman*, no longer committed to one guild or master, maybe travelling widely and finally producing his *chef d'oeuvre eleve*, demonstrating his capacity to become Master. Such a system spread across many trades, but one should recognise its outstanding achievements in the buildings, statues, and carpentry of medieval churches still used throughout Britain several hundred years afterwards. Later, the Livery companies, established in 1327, were trade associations, established from the Guilds (for example, the Goldsmiths Company) to regulate the trade and to support apprenticeships, who would learn to smelt, purify and weigh precious metals (See More, C., 1980, *Skills and the English Working Class*).

Such a growing collection of craft guilds developed, in 1563, into a national system of apprenticeship training in what was called the Statute of Articifers. This set out the nature and the conditions of apprenticeship which survived more or less into the 19th century. These included the requirement that the Master Craftsman should have no more than three apprentices and that the apprenticeship should last for seven years. Thus there was developing a more secure and satisfying 'career path' for members of the working class.

However, the Act was repealed in 1814, the beginning of our period. The reasons would seem to arise from the growing development of the Industrial Revolution which gave rise to very different new industries such as engineering and shipbuilding characterised by their production lines. These production lines did not require the traditional craft skills, although there then grew the need for a different sort of preparation of the workers as plumbers and electricians. But, as the Paris Exhibition of 1867 revealed (*referred to in Chapter 1*), other countries such as Germany in particular were becoming more advanced than Britain because of their superior technical training, thereby challenging the prominence of the developing industrialisation of Britain.

The changing economic and industrial scene saw the development of factories using mechanisation, which diminished the need for skilled craftsmen, to be replaced with unskilled workers working the production lines. However, later in the century there was an increased need for Colleges focusing upon the technical knowledge and skills required for the new industrial scene. As reflected in lowing chapters, several such colleges evolved into the new Civic Universities turn of the century.

Apprenticeship and practical learning

More needs to be said, however, about the nature and characteristics of apprenticeship expertise. In his book, *The Case for Working with Your Hands* (2009, p. 159), Matthew Crawford (combining the expertise of both philosopher and motorcycle mechanic) describes the learning process characteristic of the apprentice under the supervision of the Master.

> The Master does the same work as the apprentice, only better. He is able to explain what he does to the apprentice because there are rational principles that govern it. Or he may explain little, and the learning proceeds by example and imitation. For the apprentice there is a progressive revelation of the reasonableness of the Master's actions. He may not know why things have to be done a certain way at first, and have to take it on faith, but the rationale becomes apparent as he gains experience.

Crawford gives detailed and graphic examples (as a motorcycle mechanic) of that learning process and of the development of practical understanding of the problem.

> What is required then is the kind of judgment that arises only from experience; hunches rather than rules. I quickly realised there was more thinking going on in the bike shop than in my previous job at the think tank.
>
> (p. 27)

(By way of explanation, one should be aware that Crawford's job at the 'think-tank' had been made possible by his degree in philosophy.)

The philosopher, Richard Sennett, in his book *The Craftsman*, explains this as follows:

> Every good craftsman conducts a dialogue between concrete practices and thinking. This dialogue evolves into sustaining habits, and these habits establish a rhythm between problem solving and problem finding.
>
> (2008, p. 9)

Characteristic, therefore, of such practical learning of the craftsman, such as the carpenter, is the development of knowledge and expertise through trial and error, through reflecting on mistakes made, and through suggestions made by a person more experienced. For example, the carpenter, through jobs assigned, would

artly through experience, knowledge of different species
vant to the different kinds of job he was (or might be)
tical problem, one hypothesises different particular solu-
in practice, bearing in mind that the practical context
previous ones. The benefit of the gradual approach to
faced, is the development of intelligent experience
understanding future problems – as explored by the
⟶er John Dewey (*see Chapter 13*).

⟶ learning, however, is also true, not only of the skilled craftsman such as
the carpenter but also (dare I say) of the amateur allotment holder, benefiting from
previous failures with the tomato crop and from the suggested explanation of those
failures by other allotment holders who are more experienced. The following year
would test out those suggestions, although there may then be other factors (such as
change of weather) which require further understandings leading to further adjust-
ments. One learns (hopefully before one gets too old) through experience, failure,
reflection, new suggestions and criticism.

Philosophical issues: the nature of knowledge

Just as, in understanding the changing educational world of the 19th century (*as
described in Chapter 1*), one needs to understand the underlying philosophical ideas
which permeated those changes and the justifications for them (those especially of
Idealism regarding the acquisition of 'culture' through the development of the 'intellect', *as developed in Chapter 10*), so too does one need to address the relevant philosophical underpinnings of practical learning, exemplified in the technical training
of apprenticeships and in the learning of the skills of the craftsman. Indeed, it would
seem that failure in this regard lies in the failure also to appreciate the role of practical learning in general education, as in the creation of new qualifications such as
the EBacc (*see Chapter 5*), thereby in the cultivation of the intellect – and indeed
in the intelligent responses to the exigencies of everyday life (a point central to the
American philosopher, John Dewey's *Pragmatism*). There is 'knowledge how' as well
as 'knowledge that'.

Indeed, Crawford (2009), the philosopher turned motor mechanic, argues that
problems arise from the separation of 'thinking' from 'doing', due in the main to
the failure to see the central part played in our understanding of the world by our
thoughtful practical engagement with it. One result from such a separation is to
extol theoretical knowledge and reasoning, and to degrade the practical within the
educational system.

Therefore, Crawford feels confident in setting the theme of his argument (p. 1)
by asserting that

> The disappearance of tools [and manual competence, p. 2] from our common
> education is the first step towards a wider ignorance of the world of artefacts
> we in habit.

Thus, in this he quotes (p. 23) no less an authority than the Greek philosopher, Aristotle:

> Lack of experience diminishes our power of taking a comprehensive view of the admitted facts. Hence, those who dwell in intimate association with nature and its phenomena are more able to lay down principles such as to admit of a wide and coherent development: whilst those whom devotion to abstract discussions has rendered unobservant of facts are too ready to dogmatise on the basis of a few observations.
>
> (*On Generation and Corruption, 316a*)

So much philosophy since Descartes 1637 starting-point *Cogito Ergo Sum* ('I think therefore I am') has seen persons as 'thinkers' rather than 'doers', building up proposition-based knowledge into theoretical understandings of the universe and of other persons within shared and readable accounts. From such accounts, behaviour or developments in the external world could be predicted or found to be mistaken. But such theoretical knowledge would often be too abstracted from the practical problems that, say, the craftsman is endeavouring to solve.

In contrast with the rationalism of a Rene Descartes is the *Pragmatism* of a John Dewey (*as shall be explained further in Chapter 13*) who insisted upon the intimate connection between 'thinking' and 'doing', thereby contrasting it with the traditional understanding and practice of formal education, namely, disconnected from experiences of home and community, from the practical and manual activity through which people engaged with experience, and from the interests which motivate the learner. Knowledge had become purely symbolic, 'stuck on' through text-books, disconnected from experience.

The good teacher, of course, would endeavour to provide the insights from such theory where it could be seen to illuminate the practices. But it would need to be grounded in the thoughtful enterprises of the active pupil or apprentice who might well be encountering problems not anticipated in the theory. Human engagement and practice certainly become the context for the more abstract theoretical thinking, but such engagement would not be able to anticipate all the complexities likely to occur in the particular practice being engaged in. The 'practitioner' has to make the best choices in the light of the evidence of different kinds at his disposal. The craftsman has to think creatively, not just to execute clear instructions.

Furthermore, it is the case that theoretical thinking at the profoundest level often arises from the puzzlement arising from practice where one is trying to make sense of something which is seen to work. Crawford (*p.22*) gives the example of classical thermodynamics.

> [The steam engine] … was developed by mechanics who observed the relations between volume, pressure and temperature. This was at a time when theoretical scientists were tied to the caloric theory of heat, which later turned out to be a conceptual dead end. The success of the steam engine contributed to the development of what we now call classical thermodynamics.

Theory and 'knowledge that' arise very often from reflection on the 'practical know-how', which is engaged in prior to theoretical reflection, endeavours to make sense of that 'know how'.

As the industrial revolution advanced, so it might be argued, there became a gradual disuse of the craft skills and of personal thinking about the practical demands and their solutions. Technological advance, which depended initially on such practical skills and thinking, gave rise increasingly to the production machine. The 'philosophy of *Pragmatism*' gave way to the 'philosophy of *Utility*', and the end product no longer reflected, as it once did, the effort, the thinking, and the personality of the craftsman. The *homo faber* had become the *homo laborans*.

Practical engagement, aesthetic appreciation and human flourishing

The practical engagement of the future craftsman was determined by the ends to be achieved – the object to be made or to be mended and the standards which were applied to doing a job well. Those standards, and the human benefit for which they were created, helped constitute the community into which the young apprentice had been initiated. That gave an ethical ethos to the distinctive life of the craftsman. The status was achieved often with a struggle to overcome problems, with the application of skills not universally held, and through expert help of a Master. To achieve status for one's skills and for work completed, in a way that others were unable to achieve, would be a strong element in the sense of personal pride – a key element in what might be called 'human flourishing'. The successful apprentice and the working craftsman would value his work as a meaningful part of his life. It would give a sense of self-reliance, the experience of agency, an essential element of what it means to be and become 'a person'. There is the connection here between the manner of thinking and the feeling of pride in the job, a caring about the job being done well.

The personal value in such occupation was enhanced by its possible aesthetic dimension, as identified and made explicit by the English writer and art critic, John Ruskin, whose influential book in 1849, *The Seven Lamps of Architecture*, provided a noble and aesthetic conception of craftsmanship, by no means to be demeaned. In so doing, Ruskin challenged the de-personalisation of work which had replaced the skilled worker and turned him into the thoughtless machine worker. That challenge was clearly reflected in one of his books.

> The great cry that rises from all our manufacturing cities, louder than the furnace blast, is all indeed for this, that we manufacture everything there except men; we blanch cotton, and strengthen steel, and refine sugar, and shape pottery; but to brighten, to strengthen, to refine or to reform a single living spirit, never enters into our estimate of advantages.
>
> (*The Stones of Venice: the Nature of Gothic, para. 12*)

But to achieve such a goal (that is, to refine or to reform the living spirit) Ruskin had to face a huge task. Many of the craftsmen no longer had the practical craft-based work within which they might be enlightened by their aesthetic perspective. Therefore, Ruskin (Oxford University and Christ Church educated) raised his educational sights more broadly to the working class, employed or unemployed, craftsmen or not. He established in the mid-seventies a Working Men's Club in London. As he said in a letter to a friend,

> I want to give short lectures to about 200 at once in turn, [to] shop decorators, and writing masters and upholsterers and masons and brick-makers and glassblowers and pottery people.
>
> (*quoted in* Sennett, 2008, p. 112)

Ruskin sought a room where such men, working or unemployed, might gather to witness pieces of art and sculptures and hand-made goods. His Oxford and Christ Church education had not disturbed his *socialist* politics and philosophy and his urgency thereby to bring an aesthetic vision to the lives of the working class.

At roughly the same time, William Morris, also an Undergraduate of Oxford, similarly saw the required reform of the depersonalised society to be achieved through making labour more pleasurable and by opening up education to the working class. Such possibilities would be made through the Socialist Democratic Federation providing not only the opportunities but also the organisation to ensure the rights and the leisure to enjoy them. In 1861, Morris gave his influential lecture on 'On Art and Socialism'. The dignity and satisfaction of labour can be gained, at least in part, through acquaintance with and enjoyment of the arts. Indeed, such arts would flourish in a society which made way for and encouraged artistic expression. Such expression would embellish the environment in which men worked and lived. The factory itself, as he argued in a further paper in 1884 entitled 'A Factory as it might be', would become a centre of learning and of artistic expression, and within the local society integrating school and workshop, theory and practice, thereby providing a basis for pleasure as a good artist as well as a knowledgeable worker.

In his book significantly entitled *William Morris, Romantic to Revolutionary* (1955), E. P. Thompson thus quotes Morris,

> I should like to see 2000 men of that stamp [working men] engaged in explaining the principles of rational, scientific socialism all over this kingdom.
>
> (p. 447)

Therefore, by contrast with the industrial developments of the late 19th century, characterised by the pursuit of machine-led productivity, Morris, as with Ruskin, held up a vision that arts could bring to its reform.

Conclusion

The chapter draws attention to the profound significance of the system of medieval apprenticeships, shaping the life of the craftsman in the 19th century – both the skills for the different trades and the sense of personal value and esteem. But the century of the Industrial Revolution saw significant changes to the economic context and thus to the life of the working man – including the values and sense of personal worth which prevailed in the apprenticeship system. It was essential, therefore, to examine more deeply the distinctive kind of knowledge, as well as the ethical context, of what was being undermined, as the country moved into the 20th century. Why should education (as 'cultivation of the intellect') not include that practical knowledge which was characteristic of the preparation of skilled workers?

This chapter, therefore, first, sought an overview of how the practical learning of apprenticeship evolved corresponding to changed economic circumstances, and how the very ideas and provisions of education changed (including, as described in Chapter 1, the development of technical skills and knowledge within their distinctive schools and colleges), leaving a legacy upon which subsequent developments were to arise.

Second, philosophical questions emerged about the educational quality of practical 'knowing how' (key to the preparation of apprentices). Is there not a misleading discrimination between 'education' and 'training', which undermines the then prevailing liberal idea of the 'cultivation of the intellect' – a discrimination which prevails to this day? To this we return in Chapters 10 and 13. None the less, the importance of technical education and training emerged, at different levels and in different kinds of institution, which would need to be embraced in the reforms of the following century.

Third, in the light of the responses from the likes of Morris and Ruskin, one sees the importance of the aesthetic and ethical character of practical learning which raises it to the realm of 'liberal learning' but which too often gets neglected.

References

Arnold, M., 1869/1932, *Culture and Anarchy*, Cambridge University Press.
Crawford, M., 2009, *The Case for Working with Your Hands*, London: Viking (The Penguin Group).
Descartes, R., 1637, *Discourse on Method*.
More, C., 1980, *Skills and the English Working Class*, London: Croom Helm.
Morris, W., 1881, 'On Art and Socialism', (ed. Holbrook Jackson, 1947).
Morris, W., 1884, 'A Factory as it might be', *Justice*, vol. 1, no. 18.
Ruskin, J., 1849, *The Seven Lamps of Architecture*, London: Routledge, 1901.
Ruskin, J., 2003, *The Stones of Venice: the Nature of Gothic*, New York: De Capo.
Sennett, R., 2008, *The Craftsman*, London: Penguin.
Thompson, E.P., 1955, *William Morris, Romantic to Revolutionary*, California: Stamford University Press.

3

PRIMARY AND SECONDARY EDUCATION FOR ALL

Introduction

Chapter 1 revealed the gradual evolution of educational provision during the 19th century from a stage in which only a minority of socially privileged people were offered the opportunity of schooling (and even smaller proportion of that minority to the exclusive higher education in the Ancient Universities), to the stage when Elementary Schooling for the poor and working class was assured by 1870 Education Act through the newly created School Boards. There thus emerged Elementary Schooling for all children up to the age of 12 and the beginnings of a national system.

This chapter describes the further evolution of the system with particular regard to the changing understanding of (and debates about) the aims and the appropriate provision of education, which bequeathed legacies that helped form future policy and practice.

Of particular importance, as explained in Chapters 1 and 2, was the growing consciousness, amongst different organisations of working-class men, of the need for education which expanded their capacity to think, to be cultured and to contribute as citizens in their newly enfranchised status. Such consciousness reflected differently perceived cultural values worth pursuing, capabilities required of a newly enfranchised population, and economic needs of society. At the same time, such (seen in the progress towards 'secondary education for all') met opposition from those of different social class who challenged the enhanced education of the working class on several grounds, including inappropriateness of Arnold's or Morris' ideals of cultivation of the intellect for those destined to work as unskilled labourers.

There had already, as has been stated, as well as an Elementary Education for all children up to age 12, also a growth of Technical Schools, Trade Schools and Commercial Schools to meet the needs of the changing economic and industrial scene, which fitted into neither the ideal of the essentially middle-class Grammar School, nor the very basic 'education' of the Elementary School. Further, there had been a remodelling of the Endowed Grammar Schools into three grades to meet different occupational needs and to reflect the subtleties of social class differentiation.

Clearly the time had come for a more comprehensive reform of educational provision as a whole, outside that provided for the social minority served by the Public Schools. Things had moved on since the Report of the Newcastle Commission. Such a relation of comprehensive reform would need to think deeply about the different aims of the educational system, about the relationship of such aims to economic needs, and about the possible differentiation of those aims to the social background of the pupils to be taught. There was seen to be the need for another Royal Commission, this time on 'Secondary Education'.

Bryce Commission into secondary education 1895

An increasing number of School Boards, established following the 1870 Education Act, had managed to develop 'higher standards' in the Elementary Schools under their authority, which qualified them as 'Higher Grade Schools', thereby affecting the conception of their 'elementary status', as is reflected in the large Victorian buildings still to be seen in major industrial cities of England. They seem to belong to a different species from that of the Elementary Schools from which they had arisen prior to the 1870 Act. The number of pupils seeking to remain at the Elementary Schools in order to reach those 'higher standards' was rising rapidly, where subjects such as science could be studied, supported financially by the Science and Art Department. According to the subsequent Bryce Commission Report, the number of pupils aged 14–15 had risen to over 50,000 by 1894. Such was the significance of this expansion, that what were originally Elementary Schools came to be designated as Higher Grade Schools. By 1895 there were as many as 67 Higher Grade Schools with nearly 25,000 scholars (see Simon, 1965, p. 179 *for details*), some aiming to move into Higher Education, soon to be made possible through the development of the Civic Universities.

Hence, evidence quoted in the Bryce Commission Report of 1895 (vol. VII, 162–3) from the headmaster of Leeds Higher Grade School, which had been visited by the Commission, was that

> This higher grade school represents a new educational movement from below, and a demand from new classes of the population for Secondary Education which has sprung up in a few years.

However, as often is the case when radical changes take place, there was opposition from some of the Endowed Grammar Schools (including Manchester Grammar School), which were facing opposition from these newcomers to Higher-Grade education with their lower fees and efficient teaching (see Simon, 1965, p. 180–1). There was a clear view amongst many powerful people, with support in Parliament, that there needed to be a clear distinction between Elementary (now including Higher

Grade) and Grammar School education in terms of qualifications and of content of what was taught. One solution proposed by the Royal Commission on Elementary Education in 1888 was that the upper grades of the Elementary Schools should provide a different sort of education for those staying at school, namely, technical and commercial instruction and preparation for the new kinds of industry emerging especially in the northern cities, to which they would transfer by the age of 15.

Thus three issues were emerging: first, need for clearer definition of Secondary Education for those leaving school at age 16 and 18; second, higher form of Elementary School (Higher Grade Schools) to accommodate those capable of technical and work-related education and who would leave school at 15 or 16, thereby better prepared for such work; and third, very basic education (especially in literacy and numeracy) for those who leaving for work at 14. Already we see germs of the system which was to develop, namely, primary schools until age 11, followed by Secondary Schools for some and Technical Schools for others, alongside the Grammar Schools for more-able middle class, possibly *en route* to the new Universities. But also, for purposes of this book, we see emerging different understandings of what education means for different children, who would be institutionalised in different kinds of school.

Moreover, behind such divisions in schooling were assumptions about the latent abilities of young people, determined by intrinsic ability associated with the social class from which they came – assumptions which fitted the kinds of employment which were available in the industrial world into which they would be entering.

According to the Secondary Teachers' Association, the Higher Grade Schools

> should be confined exclusively to higher primary work, … and their aims should be of a definitely practical character, as intended for hand-workers rather than head-workers.
>
> (see Banks, O., 1955, p. 16)

A complicating background to these developments within the emerging system was the tension between the School Board's and the Church's responsibility for Elementary Schools, following the establishment of School Boards by the Education Act of 1870. The former's schools were expanding considerably at the expense of the latter's, thereby undermining a feature of Elementary Schools since their establishment, namely, that of the promotion of a Christian ethos in this more secular environment. This tension would remain a background to reform until finally resolved under the 1944 Education Act. But it raises philosophical issues about the nature and place of religion as an element in educational formation and provision – an issue to be examined in Chapter 7.

Furthermore, the financing of Elementary Schools (local rates for School Board Schools, charitable funding for Church schools, and grants from the Science and Art Department for Higher Grade Elementary Schools) increased difficulties in a system which was supposed to be equitable for all. Gradually, through a complicated process, newly formed administrative units of School Boards were undermined in favour of control by County Councils – the beginnings of local democratic responsibility for public education. Part of the impetus for such democratic responsibility came from representatives of the working class, in particular the Trades Union Congress, in the demand for 'the common school' as intrinsic to its educational ideals, and for clear division between primary and secondary phases. In a Memorial to the Bryce Commission, the TUC defined Secondary Education as that which follows (but continues) Primary or Elementary Education, and argued that all children should be educated in a

> common school' and thus realise and enjoy in their youth common interests and pursuits as the children of one country.
>
> (Bryce Commission, vol. V., 494–8)

What was required of a reformed educational system was *equality of opportunity* which, according to the Resolution of TUC Report of 1896, required the abolition of the scholarship system which

> provided Secondary Education only for the very small proportion of the workers' children who can come to the top after severe competition with their school fellows.

On the other hand, there was not total unanimity from those who were seeking a fair and inclusive system. Sidney Webb, Chairman of the London Technical Education Board, sought a scholarship system whereby the ablest boys and girls aged 11 to 13 in public Elementary Schools could be picked by competitive examination for two to five years' higher education. That, so it was argued, would enhance the efficiency of the educational system in serving the needs of the State.

Education Act, 1902 and developing arguments

Therefore, let us see for the purposes of this book, as we approach the Education Act of 1902, the underlying ideas about education and its purposes, which arose from the discourse within and around the Bryce Commission, and which would inform that legislation and the shape of education to come.

First, educational opportunities needed to be expanded and improved for all young people, especially in Elementary Schools, aided by (i) abolition of all fees in Elementary and Secondary Education, (ii) raising of the school-leaving age, and (iii) (according to Sidney Webb, 1901, 13–15), 'a really effective national minimum of education'.

Second, revolutionary changes were required for democratic responsibility for the different provisions (regional and local) within an overall system, in place of that currently and partly provided by independent School Boards. The time had come 'to complete the work of 1870 by giving in every district the same democratic control over education' (33rd. TUC Report, 1900, 119–20). Thus, London County Council (LCC) became a Local Education Authority (LEA) with the abolition of the London School Board – unchanged until 1965 with the creation of the new Inner London Education Authority (ILEA).

Third, the total framework of different kinds of publicly funded education and training should come under a single Government department, headed by a Board of Education.

Fourth, a clear distinction was required between primary and secondary, with opportunity to progress to 'secondary' (perhaps aided by scholarships) through availability of a wider range of subjects or in pursuit of more technical and vocational subjects.

Fifth, those technical and vocational subjects may perhaps be more effectively taught in separate schools or colleges within the new system of secondary education.

Sixth, a scholarship system would enable working-class pupils from the Elementary Schools (but only those of 'exceptional ability') to benefit from such secondary education.

Seventh, there was need for a reappraisal of the religious influence within this evolving system – against some opposition (from the secularist reformers) to religion-based schools being equally financed on the rates. One of the main objections to the Bill had been

> the permanent fortification of the clerical schools by throwing almost the last penny of their financial burden on to the public funds, while leaving them under ecclesiastical management.
>
> (*quoted in* Simon, 1965, p. 229)

The 1902 Act, therefore, was a first step towards dealing with these issues:

- New Local Education Authorities (LEAs) were established to administer and finance Elementary and Secondary (including Technical) Schools. By the close of 2003, 240 LEAs (that is, two-thirds) had been established.
- Church schools would now be on the rates, although problems were perceived in reconciling such religious commitment with the secular ethos of many reformers.
- Relation between Elementary and Secondary ('advanced instruction for the few') was vaguely resolved, though awaiting debate on practical implementation and on what that could possibly mean. The Secondary Code, for example, following the Act, simply referred to 'an education up to and beyond age 16 which offers general education, physical, mental and moral through a graded course of instruction of wider scope and more advanced degree than that offered in Elementary Schools' (see Simon, 1965, p.240).

The Act and subsequent regulations did not say anything very significant about the nature of that education to be pursued in Elementary Schools up to age 14 or Secondary Schools up to ages of 16 or 18. Indeed, the exact nature of the Higher Elementary Schools (an extension which initially remained part of Elementary Schools and intended to fit pupils for certain classes of employment) remained unresolved in relation to Secondary, despite much debate and discussion within and without Parliamentary Consultative Committees. Furthermore, it was not until 1907 that free places were made available for candidates from the Elementary to transfer to Secondary without the continued use of the scholarship system which had demanded 'exceptional ability'. But, even there, it was argued by Tawney (1922), in his 'plea' for *Secondary Education for All,*

> The truth is that the free place system, though useful in making a break, if a small one, in the walls of educational exclusiveness, was really the product of an age in which secondary education was regarded as an exceptional privilege to be strained through a sieve, and reserved, as far as the mass of the people were concerned, for children of exceptional capacity.
>
> (p. 83–84)

Looking to the future: issues emerging

Therefore, several issues emerged which affected what could count as 'education' and which would not be resolved until the 1944 Education Act (but then only partly).

First, little attention had been given to the place of practical and technical knowledge within the collection of subjects of the traditional Secondary Schools' curriculum, resulting in an uneasy relationship between the Higher Level Grades, which had developed within the Elementary System, and their new status in the Secondary. One conclusion of Chapter 2 was that a comprehensive account of intellectual and cultural development would be deficient without such practical as well as theoretical intelligence.

Second, the existing Secondary Schools (particularly Grammar) were concerned about (and resistant to) the possibly large influx of Elementary School pupils, ill-prepared for traditional Secondary curriculum in terms of relevant knowledge or intellectual training. Extension of Secondary, therefore, would require, also, reforms to what came to be called Primary.

Third, what continued to shape educational thinking and arrangements was the social class discrimination inherited from the rigid division of schools into Public, Endowed Grammar, and Elementary, still affecting perceptions of what different classes of pupils were capable of aspiring to or of achieving. As the Schools Enquiry Commission Report of 1868 (Vol. 1, p. 93) had put it, each social class required its own, differentiated education:

> Education has become more varied and complex … the different classes of society, the different occupations of life, require different teaching.

Hence, the growing cry for greater equality (showing *Socialist* influence – see Chapter 10). To quote Tawney,

> The purpose of the educationist is to aid their [*all children's*] growth. It should be easy to regard them, not as employers or workmen, or masters and servants,

or rich or poor, but merely as human beings. Here, if anywhere, the spirit of equality might be expected to establish its kingdom. Here, if anywhere, it should be possible to forget the tedious vulgarities of income and social position, in a common affection for the qualities which belong to man himself, and in a common attempt to improve them by cultivation.

(Tawney, 1931/38 *revised edition*, p. 141)

Hence, Tawney (1931, p. 15) talks of their 'common humanity a quality which is worth cultivating'. Such powerful and influential sentiments, though coming from a spokesman for Socialism, had echoed what was argued by statesmen of different occupation. Thus, H. A. L. Fisher, Vice Chancellor of Sheffield University, but appointed as President of the Board of Education, said in his speech in Newcastle in 1916 that

Education dispels the hideous clouds of class suspicion and softens the asperities of faction… The sense of the value of education as an end in itself, as one of the constituent elements in human happiness, is now widely spread amongst the manual workers of the country.

(Times Educational Supplement, 19.4.1917)

Fourth, the Secular Education League, formed in 1907, argued that 'teaching of religion was not the responsibility of the state' and should not be subsidised by the rates. It called for a 'national system of education, elementary and advanced, free and secular, and under complete popular control' (*Justice, April 1908*). This issue, despite constant arguments from both secularists and the Churches, was not resolved until the 1944 Education Act.

Fifth, however and above all, there were unresolved philosophical issues concerning the meaning of 'education', or the 'human flourishing' to which Tawney and Fisher implicitly referred, and the forming thereby of an educated and tolerant citizenry to be achieved through the school's life and curriculum. Such issues and questions necessarily continued to shape educational policy and practice. The Fisher Act of 1918, therefore, took the system, and therefore concept, of education further along the path to one that would seem to be fair and profitable to most interests.

More, however, was still required as reflected in two major reports. The first, namely, the Hadow Report, 1926 (*Report of the Consultative Committee on the Education of the Adolescent*), argued for a clean break between Secondary and Primary schooling, reflected in the lines

There is a tide which begins to rise in the veins of youth at the age of 11 or 12. It is called by the name of adolescence

The second was the Spens Report, 1938, *Secondary Education with Special Reference to Grammar Schools and Technical High Schools*, in 1938.

Approaching a partial resolution of the problems

The Spens Report (1938) reflects at length (nearly 500 pages) the debates which were to overcome many of the difficulties which were unresolved by the 1902 Act and which embodied conflicting understanding of what 'education' entailed for young people. In so doing, it helped to prepare the way for the 1944 Education Act which became a further major step in providing an education which would seem to be relevant to the changing social and economic context, and therefore to the educational thinking arising from that context, illustrating the declaration by McCulloch, given in the Introduction to this book:

> It is hard to understand education without recognising its historical charac-teristics... The interplay of past and present has special resonance when we are dealing with education. It offers us ample opportunity to make use of the wisdom of the past.

The key features of the Spens Report might be summarised as follows:

First, Clear division at 11 between 'primary' and 'secondary' (as recommended by Hadow).

Secondary schooling would be characterised by the range of subjects which were understood to develop the intellect in its different capacities (or 'faculties') so as to be able to exercise judgement on issues of human significance. Such capacities would be realised developmentally through the acquisition of key ideas or concepts. In many respects, this was the idea of a 'liberal education' as articulated by Matthew Arnold (1866/1932), indicated as such by Spens (p. 59). In its broadest understanding, it was akin to traditional conception of education of the Public and Endowed Grammar Schools, though without primacy given to Latin. Such a broadly conceived curriculum was seen to be acceptable to most pupils at the age of 11, not just to a few scholarship winners or products of the Public Schools. It could be pitched at a level of understanding reached by the pupils at the age of 11.

Second, Reform of the Primary Curriculum

There was need for change in preparation for Secondary, with more than bare minimum of literacy and numeracy being attained, although Sidney Webb's (1901) recommendations for 'a really effective national minimum of education' was not taken up. But it would require a gradual preparation for the broader intro-duction to human development than had hitherto been the case in Elementary Schooling and thus an initiation into what was to follow at post-primary level.

Third, Different capacities and motivations should be recognised by age 11

It would be appropriate to have three types of school: *Grammar* for contin-uation of the liberal ideal up to age 18 for pupils likely to intend to advance to University; *Modern* for those leaving at 16 for employment or specialist training;

Junior Technical (linked to Technical Colleges) for those preparing for particular industries such as engineering or building. Such practical learning had evolved through apprenticeships, and then through technical, trade, commercial, and industry-related schools. But it was intended to sit alongside aspects of the 'liberal tradition'.

Fourth, Multilateral Schools

Recognition was given to the difficulty of making available three different kinds of Secondary School in more remote areas, and so it was seen necessary to develop some 'Multilateral Schools' which would need to cope with different attainments through streaming.

Fifth, Importance of more practical and technical learning

This would apply also within Grammar and Modern Schools as an important part of the development of intellect. For many it would be central to their human development, as argued by Ruskin and Morris (*see Chapter 2*), though within a broader group of subjects.

Sixth, Girls' education

Neglected in the discourses on development of education (as must have been noted so far) was specific concern for girls' education, despite influential forces within the Public School sector from such pioneers as Miss F. M. Buss' London Collegiate School (1850) and Miss Dorothy Beale's Cheltenham College for Young Ladies (1853). Girls were later allowed to enter Cambridge Local Examinations. There was gradual assimilation of girls' courses with those of boys in the new Secondary system, they too needing the general education whilst possibly supplemented by such practical subjects as 'housewifery'.

Seventh, External examinations and tests

These would set 'standards' defining progress and attainment. After 1850, the better boys' schools would submit entries for Indian and Home Civil Service Examinations, and later for Oxford and Cambridge Local Examinations. In 1873, the Oxford and Cambridge Local Examination Board was established with Higher Certificate for those aged 18, Lower Certificate for those aged 16. In 1879 girls were admitted to these examinations.

Reflections on the changing aims of education

This sketchy account of desirable changes to organisation and content of education, particularly as given at great length in Spens Report (arising from consultations of several Royal Commissions, responses to extension of the franchise, and different interested parties) shows how the very concept of education had been challenged and (one might say) reformed in the light of fresh evidence, social relevance and philosophical reflection. The prevailing and dominant concept of 'education' was implicitly examined, and defined not simply in terms of intellectual attainment in specific subjects but in terms of 'human fulfilment' which had several dimensions. Much emphasis, therefore, was put, for example, on the following.

(i) *Broader understanding of 'education'*

It was argued in Spens Report (*p. 56, footnote*) that education in Secondary School should be organised along the lines indicated by Matthew Arnold's understanding, in 1866. of the 'cultivation of the intellect', but should not be so confined and thereby identified only with traditional subjects, howsoever significant these might be.

> We are aware that that there are some who would limit the term education to the discipline of faculty and the culture of character by means of the more humane and generous studies, and would deny the name instruction in those practical arts and sciences by means of which man becomes a craftsman or a bread-winner. But this is an impossible limitation as things now stand. We have just seen that the training in classics may have as little liberal culture in it as instruction in a practical art.
>
> (p. 58)

Therefore, Spens Report pressed on with the inadequacy of 'culture' as an end in itself and asserts the importance of links within general education between such cultural achievement, and the arts and crafts (for example, 'applied mechanics and subjects connected with agriculture for those who lived and went to school in rural parts of the country).

(ii) *Development of citizenship as a factor in that broader understanding*

Between 1832 and 1923, five Electoral Reform Acts entirely transformed the basis of political representation – from a privilege, gradually extended, to a right for all. The 1867 2nd Reform Act nearly doubled the electorate, especially in the towns – though women's suffrage was delayed until 1918, and then only when they reached the age of 30. Much importance gradually came to be attached to the development of 'citizenship' through curriculum and ethos of the school,

> emphasising the serious character of the social and other problems which have to be faced, and at the same time insisting that, whilst there is need for enthusiasm in causes which are felt to be vital, there is need also for study or judgment.
>
> (Spens, pp. 33/34)

Such 'study or judgment' would be assisted particularly by the subject of history which was seen to bring out the general necessity of certain qualities. Hence, 'citizenship' should be part of the curriculum so that

> the youth of the country can be fitted to fulfil later duties, and to take advantage of their opportunities as citizens of a democratic state.
>
> (Spens, ditto)

(iii) *Conception of 'the whole person' (especially through language and literature)*
The development of 'distinctive human qualities and fulfilment' gave greater depth than heretofore to the learning of languages, for

> Nothing appears to develop and discipline the whole man so much as the study which assists the learner to understand the thoughts, to enter into the feelings… to appreciate the moral judgment of others … Clearness of thought is bound up with clearness of language… Refinement follows when study of literature follows study of language.
>
> (Spens, pp. 33–4)

However, there is little account in Spens Report of the importance and provision of the aesthetic dimension, articulated by the likes of William Morris and John Ruskin, as important enrichments of the lives and appreciation of (amongst others) the future craftsman. Nor does the 'moral dimension' to that conception of 'the whole man' or of 'human flourishing' receive explicit mention in the account of the future of Secondary Education, but it is no doubt implicit in the teaching of religious understanding, even though, against the background of a secular age, such religious beliefs could not be advanced as the basis for morality. Such moral understanding and approach to life would no doubt be explored through emphasis on the study of literature throughout the school.

(iv) Greater sense of equality
Moral values would be implicit in the emphasis on 'equality' both in the provision of educational opportunities and in the relationships between pupils of different backgrounds, in what Tawney had emphasised as

> a common affection for the qualities which belong to man himself, and in a common attempt to improve them by cultivation'.
>
> (Tawney, as quoted above)

Such sense of equality would be pursued through giving, as far as could be the case, more equal status between the different kinds of school and by recognising, through the different studies, the cultivation of the distinctively human qualities pertaining to everyone, even more significant now in their common citizenship. Indeed, as Joan Simon argued in her paper entitled 'The shaping of the Spens Report on Secondary Education, 1933–38', the Report was initiated

> with a view to securing equality of conditions in post-primary schools of different types.
>
> (Simon, J., 1971)

However, the Spens Report, though emphasising Secondary Education for all after the age of 11, argued that such education should take place within a tripartite system of Grammar, Technical and Modern schools – a conclusion not universally shared, especially those who were concerned about the future of the poorer pupils from the working class and who argued for a 'common school' for all pupils, where the 'common affection', referred to by Tawney (quoted above) would more likely be achieved.

Onward to the 1944 education act

Spens Report was the final one of a list of Consultative Committees which were influential in the evolution of educational thinking during the inter-war years, reflecting a style of decision-making, which itself was part of educational reflection and philosophy to be rejected in subsequent years (*as shall be argued in Chapter 8*). However, the following details of such an influential Consultative Committee may help to make this deeper educational point. The consultation lasted five years, which were needed to deliberate thoroughly the aims of education relevant to all young people throughout their developing lives, bearing in mind the evolving social and economic structures of society and the range of abilities and aspirations to be taken into account. No simple or ready-made answers would do. Argument, philosophical reflection, research and evidence were essential. To pursue such a task, the Committee of 20 members sat during that period for over 70 days in total, informed also by sub-committees which augmented expertise, digesting relevant research and evidence. Their meetings took 50 days altogether. Moreover, the Commission consisted predominantly of men and women immersed in education at different levels who were able to bring their practical experience and wisdom to the deliberations. In other words, the Committee and its processes of extensive consultation were the very embodiment of the idea of education which it endeavoured to see implemented in schools.

Despite the thoroughness of the Spens Report, vigorous debates continued about the future structure and nature of education, particularly concerning that of Secondary Education, urged on, for example, by the newly established Council for Educational Advance. A key area of dispute was whether the reshaped Secondary system should comprise 'Common' (in later nomenclature 'Comprehensive') Schools or the emerging Tripartite System of Grammar, Technical and Modern Schools as recommended by Spens Report. Such debates related, too, to the continued existence of the Public Schools within the overall provision. As Fred Clarke (1941) argued in his contribution to the ongoing debate in his influential paper, 'The Public School and the Nation', the discussions (engaged in vigorously despite the prevailing background of the World War) showed

> quite inadequate appreciation of the grim facts of the actual contemporary situation… the serious social mischief now being caused by claims on behalf of the Public Schools.

The consequence, as usual, was to create a Committee – the Norwood Committee – whose 1943 Report came down in favour of the Tripartite System on the grounds of

the 'nature of the children'. There were, it was argued, three kinds of children requi-
ing different approaches to education, namely: first, a few capable of abstract thought
and learning for its own sake; second, some more apt in the application of ideas in
technology; third, the majority who were able to engage in practical activities connected with the immediate environment. As a later commentator commented

> Seldom has a more unscientific or more unscholarly attitude disgraced the
> report of a public committee ... The suggestion of the committee seems to be
> that the Almighty has benevolently created three types of child in just those
> proportions which would gratify educational administrators.
>
> (Curtis, S. J. 1952, pp. 114–5)

The result of the Spens and Norwood Reports, and of the many debates, was the
1944 Education Act, the principal legislation of which was as follows.

First, despite the active resistance to a tripartite system from within the Labour
Party (elected in 1945), such a system became a requirement on all LEAs, which
had therefore to develop plans covering Primary and Secondary Schools, where the
education provided would be in accord with the pupils' 'ages, abilities and aptitudes'.
Indeed, a Ministry of Education Circular of 1945, entitled *The Nation's Schools*
(prepared before Labour were in power), argued strongly against Comprehensive
Schools. New Secondary Schools should be conceived as schools for working-class
children (roughly 70% of total intake)

> whose future employment will not demand any measure of technical skill
> and knowledge.

None the less, the wording of the Act was such that, at a future date, Comprehensive
Systems could be formed without major changes to the legislation – and that did begin
to occur, even though there was immediate hostility to the idea. However, despite
fairly intense criticism of the influence of the exclusivity of the Public Schools on the
Secondary sector as a whole, there was no reference to them in the legislation. One
might say, therefore, that in the main the 1944 Act left the hierarchical arrangements of
schools much as they had been: Public Schools, Direct-Grant (charging fees), Grammar,
Technical and Secondary Modern, the last three being in the 'maintained sector'.

Second, school-leaving age remained at 15 for the time being. 16 was seen to be
the desirable age, but to be postponed partly because of the post-war difficulties in
taking a large section of the age-group away from the work-force at such a time.
Compulsory schooling until age of 16 was postponed until 1972.

Third, the 'dual system' of Church and Secular schools remained, Church schools
becoming either 'Voluntary Aided' or 'Voluntary Controlled', being publicly financed
but retaining some autonomy. Chapter 7 points to the significance of these institutional arrangements for the debates about the concept of education and its relevance
to educational provision. None the less, there was meanwhile a victory for the religious lobby in that a daily act of worship would be compulsory in all schools, as also
would be some form of religious instruction, though with the right to withdraw.

There were, of course, other requirements following from the Act (for example, free milk and school meals, registration and inspection of independent schools, provision of nursery education and classes, and provision also for special educational needs), but key aspects relevant to educational values, permeating and implicit within the system, were the three above.

However, what is apparent is the lack of any overriding consideration of the aims of education, or how a concept of 'an educated person' was to shape such a divided system of Secondary Schooling – unless one counts the ill-defended assumption that, by age 11, one could identify three kinds of thinking which warranted three different kinds of school. There was also the implicit but unquestioned *Utilitarian* view of the purpose of education in terms of working and social life – being fitted for certain kinds of employment where those of low intelligence should acquire only the qualities which fitted them for relatively unskilled employment. There was no discourse, it would seem, about that personal fulfilment demanded by the working man, as described in Chapters 1, namely,

> the leisure to think, to learn, to acquire knowledge, to enjoy, to develop, in short, leisure to live,

or the opportunity to further that yearning

> for culture … the opportunities for physical and mental development, and we openly and fearlessly declare war on all that tends to keeps us riveted to the earth

or indeed for the qualities and knowledge required for the participation as citizens in the more democratic society arising from the widening of the franchise.

It was as though the politicians and civil servants within the new Ministry of Education had never heard of, let alone read, Matthew Arnold, William Morris or John Ruskin – the influential prophets, from the previous century, of a distinctively human life, but now forgotten.

Final victory for the common school

The hopes of those, who had argued strongly for the Common School, were not to be vanquished. The argument then still seemed valid after the 1945 Election, namely, as Alice Bacon (1945, p. 126 – *Labour M.P. for N.E. Leeds*) had argued, immediately prior to the Election,

> We say that as far as secondary education is concerned, we favour multilateral schools where all children are educated in one building… We promise that if we get to power we will have a free democratic educational system on which we can build up a free and democratic country.

Such an aspiration was re-enforced by the criticism of the validity of the 11+ tests on the basis of which children were divided into three separate groups of intelligence, warranting different kinds of education as described above. The grounds for such optimism had been given by the psychologist, Cyril Burt (1933, pp. 28/9),

> The psychologist understands inborn, all-round intellectual ability. It is inherited, or at least innate, not due to teaching or training; it is intellectual, not emotional or moral, and remains uninfluenced by industry or zeal; it is general, not specific, i.e. it is not limited to any particular kind of work, but enters into all that we do or say or think. Of all our mental qualities, it is the most far reaching; fortunately, it can be measured with accuracy.

However, the validity of this central foundation for the tripartite system came to be questioned as early as the 1950s on several quite different grounds.

First, doubts were cast by Philip Vernon (1952 and 1959) on the validity of the so-called 'measurement with accuracy' because it could be shown that IQ might be raised at least 14 points simply through systematic coaching – and, indeed, that is what began to happen at many schools and homes (where training text-books were made available by anxious parents – including those of this author). Indeed, in the Foreword to the Newsom Report (1963) *Half Our Future*, Edward Boyle, Secretary of State, said

> The essential point is that all children should have an equal opportunity of acquiring intelligence and of developing their talents and abilities to the full.

The second ground for doubt was, thinking back to Alice Bacon's declaration above, that through a common school experience all pupils should come to appreciate more fully the common humanity and shared values of diverse people, so essential to a democratic community.

The third ground for doubt was that even those, who were deemed to be less intelligent, would benefit from, and be inspired by, that 'cultivation of the intellect', in its different 'faculties' – the inheritance from the idealism captured by the likes of Matthew Arnold (1866) and articulated so passionately in the late 19th century by the different working men's groups calling for the opportunity to learn (*see Chapter 1, pages xx*). They, too, could benefit from the introduction, at different levels, to that 'conversation between the generations of mankind' through which they might understand better their physical and social environment. In other words, the selection of the large majority of pupils for a distinctive schooling was not inspired by any recognisable educational thinking.

However, efforts to move to a 'comprehensive system' were not successful for more than a decade, partly through the economic caution of the 1950s, and partly through the strong lobby for retention of Grammar Schools. But a few Comprehensive Schools were established in various parts of England and Wales, significantly in London (following its post-war 'London School Plan') with the all-girls school of Kidbrooke amalgamating one Grammar, two Technical and two Modern Schools. By 1954 there were over a dozen Comprehensive Schools in England and Wales, plus eight in London, albeit through different sorts of amalgamation. By 1958 there were as many as 26 in the wider London area. But all this had to be achieved without the destruction of Grammar Schools, and thus made possible mainly by building on new housing estates or areas badly damaged by wartime bombing. In such schools the close divisions between 'three types of child' were increasingly smudged over in recognition of the different kinds of talent and of the impact of ambitious teaching. The 1958 White Paper, *Secondary Education for All: a new drive*, was half-way there in arguing, with reference to new Secondary Moderns, that there should be 'a full secondary education for each of their pupils in accordance with their ability and aptitude'.

The 1944 Act had not legislated against a Comprehensive system, and various LEAs sought permission successfully to move in that direction. As already quoted, by 1964 the Conservative Secretary of State, Edward Boyle in his foreword to the 1964 Newsom Report, *Half our Future*, wrote that

> all our children should have an equal opportunity of acquiring intelligence, and of developing their talents and abilities to the full.

The movement to Comprehensive re-organisation was sufficiently large that the Government issued Circular 10/65, not imposing any solution, but inviting all LEAs to submit plans, though without legislating exactly the model to be acceptable. At long last, too, technical education came to be recognised as much more than a 'poor second' that it had occupied in a Tripartite System. But that important development leads on to Chapter 4.

Yet in some respects the 'tripartite division' left its marks in many of the new Comprehensive Schools. A distinction between the academic and the practical was reflected in the isolation of the practical in the subject often called 'design and technology', reserved for the less academic and finally losing its place in the introduction of the English Baccalaureate in 2010.

But, in anticipation of that, it is worth quoting the Preface of Crawford's book where he refers to the consequence for American education of this separation.

> 'Shop class' [that is, practical lessons dealing with design, craft skills and technology] was once a standard part of the American school curriculum, but is less so today. The original title was intended to suggest that such technical training, though narrow in its application, may be understood as an element of education in the broadest sense: intellectual and moral formation.

Primary schools

Secondary education for all, beginning at age 11 (for the vast majority of children, though some LEAs supported Middle Schools) demanded more thought to be given to the Primary stage of education which had emerged from the Elementary Schools. The Plowden Report, 1967, for England, was briefly introduced by the Secretary of State to consider primary education in all its aspects, and the transition to secondary education.

Contemporaneously the Gittins Committee was established in Wales, producing its Report in 1968). Both Reviews gave what were seen by many conservative thinkers and practitioners as quite radical. In the words of Maurice Kogan (1987), secretary to the Plowden Committee,

> It took on the exemplary function adopted by all previous consultative committees and central advisory councils. It laid out the best practices that could be found in primary schools with a view to encouraging others to follow them.

One such practice criticised was that of intelligence testing for selection to Secondary Schools, leading to extensive streaming in the Primary Schools. In reviewing a wide range of practices, the Reports encouraged more 'active learning', the arts and music, engagement in exploration or discovery, and interactions with teachers and other pupils as part of their educational experience. There arose the phrase 'the Plowden philosophy', often associated with such 'growth theorists' as Froebel or John Dewey (*as explained in Chapter 12 on Pragmatism*), and receiving thereby the criticism of being 'child-centred', a far cry, it would seem, from the initiation into the inherited forms of knowledge. There was, therefore, a powerful reaction from the authors of the 'Black Papers', of which five were published, edited by Brian Cox and A. E. Dyson, for example, *Fight for Education* and *The Crisis in Education*, both in March (1969).

Conclusion: changing understanding of 'education'

The overall theme of this book lies in the reflection on how different understandings of 'education' arise within, and indeed drive, the changing social and economic contexts. We have seen how the gradual emergence of a national system (initially rigidly divided along social class lines) came to be more flexible and open to opportunities to those once thought to be uneducable – what the Bryce Commission referred to as 'a new educational movement from below'. Such an emergence arose from different influences.

One such influence was economic, as industrial growth and competition required a more intelligently skilled labour force. Another influence was the questioning of the prevailing belief in rigid divisions between three types of fixed intelligence measurable at the young age of 11, which relegated over 70% to the lowest level, warranting only the minimum of education. More significantly was the growing awareness of the relevance of the cultural inheritance (articulated by the likes of Arnold and Coleridge), and the aesthetic appreciation (shown by such as Morris, 1884, and Ruskin, 1849) amongst the working class – in the words of William Morris, a 'vision of a society in which labour would be pleasurable and education the right of all'.

Moreover, the shift to a more democratic idea of society through the extension of the franchise required the knowledge and skills of an active citizenry, and thus the growing sense of a 'common humanity'.

This greater awareness of individual potential, nourished by initiation into a shared and inherited culture, opened up educational possibilities and awareness, which in turn made demands on the continual reforms of the system, especially the development of Secondary Education for All. But economics would continue to play its part, as industry would require ever more sophisticated skills in the workplace. However, such practical engagement, as was argued in Chapter 2, was increasingly seen to be one further aspect of that development of intelligence, requiring special attention, as we shall see in the following chapter.

Finally, however, the changing social and economic conditions cannot be seen as the only determinants of the evolving idea of education. Throughout we have seen the influence of philosophical thinking about the nature and purpose of education – whether the Idealist conception of initiation into 'the best that has been thought and said', or whether alternatively the Utilitarian pursuit of what is useful in promoting the happiness of the greatest number, or whether in the influence of Socialist ideas concerning the common good for all citizens of whatever social class, or whether in the Pragmatism asserting the intimate connection between thought and action. These philosophical underpinning theories are referred to more explicitly in Chapter 9, before being examined more closely in Part II.

References

Arnold, M., 1866/1932, *Culture and Anarchy*, Cambridge University Press.

Bacon, A., 1945, *Labour Party Conference Report*.

Banks, O., 1955, *Parity and Prestige in English Secondary Education*, London: Taylor & Francis.

Beloe Report, 1960, *Secondary Schools Examinations other than the GCE*, London: HMSO.

Bryce Commission, 1895, *Report of the Royal Commission on Secondary Education*, London: HMSO.

Burt, C., 1933, (ed.) *How the Mind Works*, London.

Clarke, F., 1941, 'The Public school and the Nation', *Journal of Education*.

Cox, B. and Dyson, A.E., 1969, (eds) *Black Papers: I Fight for Education and II The Crisis in Education*, London: Dent.

Crawford, M., 2009, *The Case of Working with Your Hands*, London: Viking Group (The Penguin Group).

Curtis, S.J., 1952, *Education in Britain since 1900*, London.

Gittins Report, 1968, *Primary Education in Wales, Central Advisory Council for Wales Hadow Report, 1926, Report of the Consultative committee on the Education of the Adolescent*, London: HMSO.

Kogan, M., 1987, 'Plowden Twenty Years On', *Oxford Review of Education*, 13(1).

McCulloch, G., 1993, Inaugural Lecture, 'Lessons from the class of 1944', in Gordon, P., ed., *The Study of Education*, London: The Woburn Press.

Morris, W., 1884, *On Art and Socialism*, (ed. Holbrook Jackson, 1947).

Newsom Report, 1963, *Half Our Future*, London: HMSO.

Plowden Report, 1967, *Children and their Primary Schools (England)*. London: HMSO.

Ruskin, J., 1849, *The Seven Lamps of Architecture*, London: Routledge (1901).

Simon, B., 1965, *Education and the Labour Movement*, London: Lawrence and Wishart.

Simon, B., 1991, *Education and the Social Order 1940–1990*, London: Lawrence and Wishart.

Simon, J., 1971, 'The shaping of the Spens Report on Secondary Education, 1933–38', *British Journal of Educational Studies*, 25 (1).

Spens Report, 1938, *Secondary Education: with special reference to Grammar Schools and Technical High Schools*, London: HMSO.

Tawney, R. H., 1922, *Secondary Education for All*.

Tawney, R.H., 1931/1952 ed., *Equality*, London: George Allen and Unwin.

Vernon, P., 1952, 'Intelligence Testing', *Times Educational Supplement*, 2nd Jan.

Vernon, P., 1959 (ed). *Secondary School Selection*, London (see Simon, 1991, p. 220.)

Webb, S., 1901, Twentieth Century Politics, *Fabian Tract* No. 108.

4

FURTHER EDUCATION AND YOUTH SERVICE

Introduction: recognition of technical education

Links had gradually been established between Secondary (especially Modern) Schools and Technical Colleges, which themselves now came to assume greater significance with the creation of the Diploma in Technology in 1956, and when the number of full-time students at the various levels of Colleges (namely, Local, Area, Regional and now Colleges of Advanced Technology – CATs) doubled from 13,000 in 1957/8 to 31,000 in 1962/3, which was the eve of the publication of the Robbins Report on Higher Education. Indeed, not only was the rigid division within the Secondary School system getting blurred, but also was the erstwhile rigid division between Schools, Colleges and Higher Education, as the more advanced Further Education Colleges came to offer part-time degree-level work.

The greater recognition of the talent required for technical capability, and its value for the economy, would seem to have needed a World War for it to be achieved! As the Conservative Prime Minister, Anthony Eden, in a speech in Bradford, January 1956, declared

> The prizes will not go to the countries with the largest population. Those with the best systems of education will win. Science and technical skills give a dozen men the power to do as much as thousands did fifty years ago. Our scientists are doing brilliant work. But if we are to make full use of what we are learning, we shall need many more scientists, engineers and technicians.
>
> (*quote* Simon, 1991, p. 198)

The White Paper, *Technical Education* (1956), therefore, distinguished between the different levels of Technologist, Technician and Craftsman, the first normally at the newly established Colleges of Advanced Technology, together with post-graduate studies and research which was relevant to particular industries. But the greatest number of young people attending Further Education, especially at the Local Colleges, would be on apprenticeships leading to Ordinary National (ONC) or Higher National Certificates (HNC) or the City and Guilds of London Institute (CGLI) qualifications for particular industries (especially engineering) from which there would be daily release for study at Further Education Colleges, together with evening classes two days a week.

Development of concept of apprenticeship

The apprenticeship system, therefore, proved to be popular, working in partnership between the Colleges and the increasing number of employers which offered day-release for the more theoretical aspects of the practices in which the young people were engaged. Furthermore, there was gradually developed the possibility of ever more sophisticated understanding and practical competence through the award-bearing system of National and Higher National Certificates, and through the developing hierarchy of Colleges (referred to above) leading for some apprentices to degree-level work and studies.

Eventually and inevitably the very concept of apprenticeship, as that was understood in the 19th and early 20th century, began to change as businesses of various kinds would seek young people to join and benefit from training systems, in partnership with Colleges, albeit in many cases far from the 'hands-on' craft-work of the original apprenticeships. Indeed, in 1993, the Chancellor of the Exchequer, Kenneth Clarke, announced the launch of a new apprenticeship scheme, entitled 'modern apprenticeships'. These were to fund people, mostly already in work with paid jobs, who would be given the opportunity and time to attend training and study for the relevant National (OND) and Higher National (HND) Diplomas at their F.E. Colleges whilst being fully paid. The costs would be partly provided by Government grants or the *Apprenticeship Levy*. Such fully paid employees would no longer need to be under the age of 25. The scheme was a recognition of the 'in-work training' provided by members of staff in various industries and businesses, but now encouraged further by Government financial support. But research by the EDSK (2020) think-tank reported that this changed understanding of apprenticeship was open to abuse, money intended for apprenticeships being spent, for example, on 'fake apprenticeships', and on relabelled courses which previously would not have been so designated. Within the next few years, the number of apprentices so defined reached 500,000. But, most significantly and worryingly, the number of GCSE equivalent students who started apprenticeships nearly halved between 2014/15 and 2017/18. (*Guardian Newspaper report on apprenticeships, 4th Feb, 2020*).

However, concepts change (as we shall see again in Chapter 6 on Higher Education) and the same words come to mean something different as social and economic conditions change. It is hard to see, on the one hand, the young 16-year-old trainee horticultural worker, for example, with day-release and evening classes at the local Technical College, and, on the other hand, the 40-year-old banker undertaking further training at his place of employment, as both being of the same species! But both would be called apprentices and would be taking National Vocational Qualifications (NVQ) which required time and support for improving their respective performances.

The *Guardian Newspaper*, however, provided valuable examples of apprenticeships for young people which illustrated a form of learning and a different conception of education from what would normally have prevailed in the schools they had recently left:

Kelly Medley left school at 16 in 1995 with poor GCSEs. So she did a Foundation Course at College. The MD of Tops Day Nurseries was her tutor. She asked if she had any jobs. As a result, she started as an early-years apprentice at a Parkstone nursery in 1996, and made supervisor at a new Tops nursery in 2000, then deputy manager. In 2002, she moved to the Aspire training team, part of the same group as Tops. By 2007 she was a training director. She has grown with the company, which now has a chain of nurseries across south-west England. She loves watching new apprentices achieve their dreams and qualifications.

Philip Parry joined Wells Cathedral stonemasons after his GCSEs in 1996, gaining NVQ level 3 in stonemasonry. He first worked as a 'banker mason', someone who carves stone, rather than a 'fixer mason' who fixes stones to the buildings. After his apprenticeship, he represented the UK at the Skills Olympics. He worked at Wolff Stone for nearly 20 years and was now self-employed. His work varies a lot, covering everything from gravestones to fireplaces, repair work and restoration. He asserts that

> apprenticeships are the best way to learn physically how to do a job. Classroom teaching has a place but is no match for on-the-job experience.

Katrina Cliffe left school at 16 in 1999 to be apprenticed in business administration. She sought an opportunity to work in reception for a marketing recruitment business. She gained NVQ Level 2 in business, later completed a Certificate in Business with Open University, and gained two Diplomas from Chartered Institute of Marketing. She worked as Marketing Manager before going freelance, starting her own PR and marketing company that works to raise the profile of small businesses in the north of England. She employs five members of staff, including an apprentice.

Martin Price, aged 17 in1996, knew he liked taking things apart and putting them back together, and so took a mechanical engineers' apprenticeship at an automotive component manufacturer's. He learnt the basics of engineering doing NVQ level 3 and BTec. in mechanical engineering. He returned to do on-the-job training and gained HNC. He now works as Director of Operations in conjunction with In-Comm, a training provider for apprenticeships rated as outstanding by Ofsted. He sees this as a great time to be an apprentice in the engineering sector.

Emily Clarke, after an 'internship', wanting to be a civil engineer was offered an apprenticeship. She works on many different projects (e.g. 'structural inspection of a waterside quay', and 'office refurbishment', which requires working closely with people on how they want their workplaces to look). She has a mentor who guides her all the way and with whom she speaks on a daily basis. She says,

> I only wish I'd known about apprenticeships, and opportunities they bring, earlier. My main advice would be that if you get a chance to do an apprenticeship, you should jump at it. Apprenticeship hasn't just boosted my career, it's changed who I am and has given me new skills, confidence and experience.

These examples suggest a deeper awareness of personal development through practical engagement, a sense of achievement, a feeling of usefulness and a growing understanding of the world into which the young apprentices would be entering and to which they would be able to make valued contributions. One might say that they convey a broader sense of 'personal or human flourishing'. As Emily Clarke said, apprenticeship changed who she was and gave her new skills, confidence and experience. Thus apprenticeships came to convey a broader sense of what it means to be educated than what generally prevails.

Too often, in assuming the centrality of more theoretical understanding (the 'cultivation of the intellect' acquired through books and instruction) in the development of the educated person, it was easy to ignore or even to disdain the practical understanding, and to support the rigid distinction which had prevailed between 'academic' and 'vocational', reflected in different kinds of institution, or even in differently streamed classes in the Common School, or again in the demotion by the Secretary of State for Education of such subjects as 'Design and Technology' from the English Baccalaureate (EBacc) in the 'reforms' of qualifications in 2010. One definition of 'academic' in the Oxford English Dictionary is

> scholarly and by implication abstract, unpractical, cold, merely logical.

Hence, a clear distinction is often assumed, according to which school subjects are divided into 'academic' and 'vocational'. As Richard Sennett (2008, p. 11) so powerfully argues in his book *The Craftsman*.

> History has drawn fault lines dividing theory and practice, technique and expression, craftsman and artist, maker and user; modern society suffers from this historical inheritance.

Expansion of Further Education

Politically and economically it was seen to be most important to reform and to strengthen vocational education and training because of the increasing needs of industry for well-trained workers, especially engineers, in the ever more competitive world economy. In his speech at Ruskin College in 1976, the Prime Minister, Mr, Callaghan gave a paper entitled *Preparing future generations for life*, emphasising: first, basic needs which industry required; second, more positive attitudes towards industry and towards the economic needs of society; third, greater technological knowledge and know-how for living in a technological society; and, fourth, the personal qualities required for living in a changing and difficult world (*see* Crombie-White, *et al.*, 1995, p. 12).

To that end, the Government established in 1977 the Further Education Unit to advise on and to support research into the curriculum and modes of learning associated with different kinds and levels of vocational preparation, based as much as possible on research and in partnership with the major awarding bodies such as City and Guilds of London Institute (CGLI) and the Royal Society of the Arts (RSA). The Unit provided a plethora of professionally focused publications, focused on different levels of education and training and drawing upon a wide range of practitioners and researchers – for example, *A Basis for Choice* in 1977, *Beyond Coping* in 1980, and *A Common Core of skills for Vocational Preparation* in 1982. Of particular significance (because so often receiving minimal attention) was the 'pre-vocational curriculum', conceived and planned to support unemployed youth and the young 'stayers-on', for whom there seemed to be no clear objectives, and also young workers who had achieved so little at school. With respect to the last group, Adult Literacy and Basic Skills Unit's 1993, report showed that

> screening of 10,000 students in further education colleges revealed that almost 4 in 10 would need some additional help with basic skills if they were to get a qualification at NVQ Level 2.
>
> (*cited in* Crombie-White *et al.*, 1995, p. 10)

Thus Further Education now had its own very active research and curriculum development unit serving Colleges and their teachers at different levels, helped by its Regional Curriculum Bases, and in particular addressing problems of underachievement which the traditional system of schooling had failed to address.

Expansion of qualifications

A further and later solution to the problems raised by the Prime Minister was to create a parallel system of qualifications by which students might progress up the vocational ladder, even to degree level. In 1986, the National Council for Vocational Qualifications (NCVQ) was set up with the idea of reforming the vocational qualifications framework by setting standards across a wide range of now National Vocational Qualifications (NVQ) at levels I to V, and, as far as possible, reflecting equivalences with the already existing General Certificate of Education framework, established after World War II (but to be 'reformed' into the General Certificate of Secondary Education in 1988). Thus, for example, within each of the apprenticeship schemes, was created a marked-out progression through different levels of achievement into degree level work at Levels 5–7 – equivalent to Foundation, Bachelor and Masters Degrees respectively, thereby blurring the distinction between Further and Higher Education.

It is, of course, difficult to draw certain conclusions about the consequences of these reforms, but evidence does suggest that they were having an effect. In the six years from 1986/87 to 1992/93, the percentage of 16 year olds participating full-time in education moved from 45% to 75%, of 17 year-olds from 30% to 55%, of 18 year-olds from 15% to 45% (DFE, 1993).

None the less, Government's continuing concern for the role of Further Education and the development of work-related knowledge and skills gave rise to the 1988 White Paper, Employment for the 1990s, which promoted the establishment of Training and Enterprise Councils (TECs), or Local Education Companies (LECs) in Scotland, to address what were still perceived to be: first, inadequate vocational education and training for craft, technician and supervisory and middle management levels; second, lower standards of attainment than in competitive nations; third, responsibility for vocational training on employers. Finally, therefore the Government endorsed, in 1991, Foundation Learning Targets, originally proposed by the Confederation for British Industry in its 1988 paper, Towards a Skills Revolution. According to these, by 1997, 80% of young people were to reach NVQ Level II by 1997, and 50% to reach NVQ Level III by 2000.

Changing conception of education?

The TECs, therefore, were given the task of setting 'training standards', namely, the *National Targets for Education and Training* (NTETs), as had been recommended by the CBI. These were to be divided into two: Foundation Learning Targets (FLTs) and Lifetime Learning Targets (LLTs). The former specified what percentage of young people should reach different NVQ levels by what dates. The latter specified, for example, that 50% of all employees should be involved in some form of training whilst employed, and that by 2000 50% of the workforce should be qualified at least to NVQ Level III.

Hence, we are witnessing here a changed language of 'education', one shaped by precise targets, defined by a Government agency and permeating the whole of post-16 education and training. Certainly, as argued above, there is a problem to be resisted of the sharp divide between the 'academic' and the 'vocational'. But now there seemed to be a tendency to overcome that divide by reducing the liberal tradition to the vocational one, through the use of a language of increasingly behaviourally defined 'standards' or 'performance indicators', which themselves become the 'targets'.

As we shall see later, in Chapter 8, that language of 'targets' and 'performativity' began heretofore to influence educational policy, planning and practice – indeed, the very language and meaning of 'education'. Here we simply need to note the rapid development of Further Education, and the increased regard for it by Government, and more widely, in the insistence upon the responsibility of the system of education, generally speaking, for the health of the industrial economy and thereby of society.

However, we have already seen indications of how such a divide between the 'academic' and the 'vocational' (between the inherited tradition of liberal education and the focus on economic outcomes) might be overcome, namely, through the incorporation of a broader understanding and questioning of the social context and responsibilities in which the work-related skills and knowledge might, and should, be seen. As we saw in the earliest chapters, the plea from the working men, engaged as apprentices, was that they needed the time and opportunities also to think, to reflect, to learn and thereby to act responsibly as citizens in their newly enfranchised status.

In some respect, the development of TVEI (Technical and Vocational Education Initiative) in the late 1980s was such a response, with emphasis on the use of the latest technology (namely, computers), and with research led by 'teacher researchers' rather than outsiders, with a view to opening up a wider vision of education through the new technology. Furthermore, we saw in the brief accounts of the five young apprentices how a tradition of constant reflection on practice, promoted by experienced mentors, encouraged not only a deeper understanding of the practice but also greater sense of personal fulfilment and social awareness. There was more to the *educational* development than could be captured in the NVQ standards and targets.

Youth centres and youth work

Easily forgotten in the consideration of the Further Education is the part played by the network of Youth Centres, partly, no doubt, because they generally speaking are not engaged in teaching towards nationally recognised awards and therefore get excluded from what is understood as a distinctively *educational* vision and its institutional arrangements. However, according to the National Youth Agency in 2010, 28% of all 13–19 year-olds were in contact with some form of Youth Service, many of them from the most desperate backgrounds in terms of family breakdown and potential abuse (HoC, 2010:9). Such centres provided safe places where young people could go in the evenings or weekends to seek advice and support, and to engage in various life-enhancing activities.

Precisely, however, because they did not fit easily into the overall educational framework (defined increasingly by standardised assessment targets within national systems of certification), they suffered worst from the cuts to the education budget in 2010. In some local authorities, there was 100% closure. The Lammy Report (2012), on the August Riots of 2011 in North London and elsewhere, put the blame for the wide-scale nature of the riots partly on the massively decreased numbers of Youth Centres where young people could mix socially in a safe and supervised environment.

Immediately previous to those riots, the National Youth Agency had said in its evidence to the House of Commons Select Committee concerning the Youth Service,

> Its distinctive characteristics include the voluntary engagement of young people, young people's active involvement in developing provision, the use of informal education as the primary method of youth engagement and an approach to provision that is responsive to young people's preferences.
>
> (HoC, 2010:9)

As one young person said, in giving evidence to the Select Committee,

> I felt that no one cared, but the youth centre, no matter what age you are when you walk in, never turns you back. It got me interested in music again after suffering from my drug addiction … it was a full-on, life changing experience for me.
>
> (ibid:15)

Another teenage account is worth quoting in full to give the essence of the distinctive educational experience of those who, though apparently failing at school, found salvation through the distinctive educational experience of the Youth Service.

> Ashby Youth Club was a big part of me whilst being aged 13–18. It kept me safe and… from getting myself and my friends into trouble. But it wasn't all about being kept off the streets. At the age we were we didn't care about anything and found it hard to communicate with parents and teachers. When it felt like the whole world shut you out there was always Jenny that you could just go to talk about anything in the world and she would be more understanding and give you best advice any could give. A lot of people called her their second mum (she was to me). There was always the education side of being at a youth club, too, learning the things we didn't really learn at school and being able to do projects with other people and learning how to really work as a team.
>
> (*quoted in* Pring, 2013, p. 171)

Such flexibility of approach is even more typical of the 'detached youth worker' who would work with teenagers, not in a youth club setting, but in their context of streets or parks, integrating with them and respecting where the young people (often in trouble and possibly members of street gangs) were mentally in their social perceptions, in their aspirations (or in the lack of them), and in the sources of their often violent and anti-social behaviour. To develop their understanding of themselves, of the alternative possibilities open to them and of a positive way out of the self-destructive form of life, would be a necessary initial stage in an *educational* process, guided by a mentor who could see the possible routes into a healthier form of life. In 2004, Joseph Rowntree Foundation funded research entitled *Reaching Socially Excluded Young People: a national study of street-based youth work*. Graeme Tiffany (2007) gives a comprehensive and illustrated account of the distinctive educational expertise and practice of such 'detached' youth workers and of their not-to-be-forgotten place in the educational enterprise. Central to this awakening educational process is an appreciation of where the young people are in their views and values, and in the beginning of a dialogue which will help them to articulate their perspectives on life in its different characteristics, namely:

> the ways of understanding the world that *they* bring and the benefits that *they* ascribe to their involvement; it puts them at the centre of a process that they own. Workers show respect for young people's power and control over their own lives, and negotiate with them how they want to be involved, what issues they want to explore and what needs they want to be met.
>
> (Tiffany, 2007, p. 4)

Conclusion

Further Education is crucial to understanding, not only the evolving nature of the educational system in the 20th century but also the evolving and controversial understanding of the very concept of 'education'. Is this an example of McCullock's words in the Introduction to this book?

> It is very hard to understand education without recognising its historical characteristics… The interplay past and present has special resonance when we are dealing with education.

FE grew massively in importance in reaction to the need for a better trained workforce within a competitive world economy, which to some extent dominated the political discourse about the need to improve the educational system. We saw in Chapter 3 how, at the Industrial Exhibitions in Paris in 1867 and elsewhere, other countries were better prepared for the newly developing industrial world as a result of their investment in skills and technical training. Clearly Britain, if it were to maintain its position in the ever more competitive industrial world, had to invest both thought and planning into improving the skills and knowledge base of its industries. That liberal education tradition, as inherited from the 19th century, would not seem able to do that. What constituted an 'educated person' needed to be reconceived.

Hence, the rapidly developing skills and technology preparation was closely related to Further Education provision, encouraging a ladder of progression from elementary skilled labour to a profounder understanding of, and the capacity for, an ever more sophisticated world of technology. This was rapidly achieved through reforms of Secondary Education, the creation of Technical Colleges and Institutions, and ladders of opportunity to improve the qualifications of those who were less successful academically at Secondary School. As the once Secretary of State for Education, Sir Kenneth Baker, wrote in his 'new vision for secondary education'

> When students are given the opportunity to learn through their hands as well as their brains, the immediate and practical become part of their lives and their passion for learning is engaged. Through working with materials like metal, wood and plastics, and by working on projects and in teams, students quickly appreciate how vital it is to master mathematical and linguistic skills.
>
> (Baker, 2013, p. 11)

One can see emerging a broader sense of 'education' which addressed a wider understanding of personal fulfilment, such as the satisfaction to be found in ultimate employment, or in the development of a style of life which gives a sense of purpose. Developing such a sense would apply equally to the process through which the underprivileged, assisted by the youth worker, might gain insight into their own lives and the possibilities of escape and progress – the deeper sense of personal development through practical engagement, a sense of achievement, a feeling of usefulness, a growing understanding of the world one is to inhabit.

Education might then be seen in the words of Mr Callaghan's 1970 Paper as 'preparing the future generation for life' (not for examinations as such). And such preparation requires the development of both the capacity to think and the capacity to act intelligently.

However, the question at the heart of education remains, as re-iterated by Sir Christopher Ball in the Foreword to the RSA Report by Roger Crombie-White, *et al.* in 1995, *14–19 Education and Training: Implementing a Unified System of Learning*,

> How, in the face of all other demands upon young people, and alongside the pressures for a better trained workforce, can we help them become more human?

Such considerations, of profound philosophical significance, bring to the fore an understanding of 'education' as what might be referred to as 'human flourishing', not reducible to being intellectually clever or practically intelligent.

Such a notion of human flourishing has not been captured in this account so far, crucial though it is. More needs to be said, for example (back to the work of Arnold, Morris and Ruskin referred to in Chapter 3) of the aesthetic dimension to an appreciation of the world which we dwell in or indeed create. But the 'life worth living' (the 'becoming more human') must surely have a moral framework, the development of which should be seen as central. That question puts at the centre of each individual's programmes of learning the exploration of what it means to be human, and how everyone, in their diverse ways, can be given the opportunity to develop that humanity to the fullest. The aim must be to help each person define the quality of life worth pursuing in economic, social, psychological, aesthetic, and emotional terms, and to find a way through the multitude of choices, within a broad framework of moral principles appropriate to a democratic and caring society.

References

Baker, K., 2013, *14–18: A New Vision for Secondary Education*, London: Bloomsbury.

Ball, C., 1995, 'Foreword', Crombie-White, *et al.* (see below).

Callaghan, J., 1976. *Preparing Future Generations for Life*, Oxford: Ruskin College.

Crombie-White, R., Pring, R., Brockington, D., 1995, *14–19: Education and Training: Implementing a Unified System of Training*, London: RSA.

DFE, 1993, Participation in Education by 16–19 year olds in England, *Statistical Bulletin* 6/93.

EDSK, 2020, *Runaway Training (a think-tank providing new perspectives on education and training)*.

Employment Dept., 1988, *Employment for the 1990s*, London: HMSO.

HoC, 2010, *House of Commons Select Committee on Youth Service*, London: HMSO.

Lammy Report, 2012, *Out of the Ashes: Britain After the Riots*, London: HMSO.

Pring, R., 2013, *The Life and Death of Secondary Education for All*, London: Routledge.

Reeves, M., 2011, *Unpublished Memoirs: The Life and Thought of Marjorie Reeves*, Lampeter: The Edwin Mellen Press.

Roberts, M. and Pring, R., 1916, *A Generation of Radical Educational Change*, London: Rouledge.

Sennett, R., 2008 *The Craftsman*, London: Penguin Books.

Simon, B., 1991, *Education and the Social Order 1940-1990*, London: Lawrence and Wishart.

Tiffany, G., 2007, *Reconnecting Detached Youth Work: Guidelines and Standards for Excellence*, London: Federation for Detached Youth Workers.

5

THE SHIFTING SANDS OF QUALIFICATIONS

Beginning of a national system

Prior to the 1944 Education Act, there was no national system of qualifications for all pupils. The minority of pupils who attended the Public Schools and the Grammar Schools would take the Higher Certificate examinations at the age of 18 and the Lower Certificate examinations at the age of 16 – a system established by the Oxford and Cambridge Local Examinations Board in 1873. The Government had no influence or control over them. Following the 1944 Education Act, however, and the commencement of Secondary Education for All, so there was seen to be a need for school-leaving qualifications for the many now staying at school to 16 and many of those to 18.

Therefore, in 1951, there was established the General Certificate of Education (GCE) – Ordinary Level at age 16 and Advanced Level at age 18 – intended for pupils who had successfully moved into the Grammar Schools, following the 11+ transition from Primary Education. However, (as noted by Chitty, 2004, p. 27) the success of pupils in Secondary Modern Schools, which also entered some pupils for the GCE, despite their failures at 11+,

> exposed the fallibility of the 11+ selection process. It was now becoming increasingly difficult to sustain the argument that a child's intellectual capacity was *wholly* or *mainly* due to something as fixed as genetic endowment.

With the gradual expansion of educational opportunities from the 19th century, as shown in preceding chapters, and also with the eventual raising of the school-leaving age to 16 in 1972 (ROSLA), so there was a need to make school-leaving qualifications more widely available to reflect what pupils, even those deemed to be of low ability, had achieved. Reference was made in Chapter 3 to the creation and development of the Certificate of Secondary Education (CSE) as a subject-based leaving-qualification for those in the Secondary Modern Schools, or indeed in the newly created Comprehensive Schools who were not deemed able to sit for the General Certificate of Education (GCE). However, the CSE was so graded that a subject at the top grade was to be seen as *equivalent* to a pass in the GCE in that subject.

Furthermore, both GCE and CSE introduced 'Mode 3' assessment, whereby one or more schools would design their own local syllabuses and assessments, verified by external moderators responsible to the Regional Examination Board. 'Mode 3' was seen initially to be particularly suitable for secondary science in order to reflect the objectives of the teaching – popular when curriculum innovation flourished partly in response to the raising of the school-leaving age in the early 1970s.

This rather complex system of two different awards at age 16, which helped to preserve the tri-partite system of school organisation within the newly developing Comprehensive Schools, could be but a step towards further reform.

Need to respect practical and vocational education

The following decades witnessed a constant struggle to reconcile the academic/vocational divide – a struggle between those who were anxious not to undermine the academic studies, reflected in the GCE qualifications, and those who sought to promote more practical and vocational learning, partly in respect for the achievements of the less academically able, and partly because of employment and economic relevance of more job-related learning, which was particularly urgent with the raising of the school-leaving age. Must there be such an academic/vocational divide in the system of education, reflected in its qualifications? To refer once again to the indictment of Richard Sennett (2008, p. 11),

> History has drawn fault lines dividing theory and practice, technique and expression, craftsman and artist, maker and user; modern society suffers from this historical inheritance.

Such problems had been anticipated when, in the late 1970s, the Further Education Unit (FEU) was established in the Department of Education and Science (DES) with the initial task of addressing the problem of the education of young people who were failing within the academically oriented curriculum of secondary schools. The question to be asked was:

> what counts as a general education for a growing number of young people, alienated by past failure, disillusioned with education as it has been experienced, ignorant of what future employment had in store – but recognising that learning mattered?

(Pring, 1997, p. 32)

A key document from the FEU (1979) was therefore significantly entitled *A Basis for Choice*, aimed at those who were not succeeding in courses leading to the mainstream qualifications. It challenged many of the pre-conceptions about the dominant educational aims of the traditional curriculum and especially the learning processes towards the achievement of those aims. In the light of the FEU's concerns and analysis, various courses developed in Secondary Schools and Further Education leading to such qualifications as the Certificate of Pre-Vocational Education (CPVE) in 1983 and, in 1986, the National Vocational Qualifications (NVQ) at 5 progressive levels which would accredit prior learning in the workplace – for example, in the Youth Opportunity Programme (YOP), commenced in 1978, and in the Youth Training Scheme (YTS), which succeeded YOP in 1983.

However, there was an increasingly widespread feeling that this wider vision of educational aims should be incorporated within the mainstream curriculum. For that purpose, the Technical Vocational and Educational Initiative (TVEI) was introduced in 1983 into the 14–19 curriculum, initiated by the Manpower Services Commission (MSC) to stimulate work-related education and greater relevance to post-school life. Eventually there were 65,000 pupils in as many as 600 schools and colleges participating in TVEI schemes (*see* Chitty, 2004, p. 50). Its specific features were: first, it focused on the practical mode in which most people learn; second, personal and careers guidance was given central place; third, communication skills were highlighted; fourth, engagement was encouraged in activities which enhanced social, political and economic awareness; fifth, recognition was given to information technology in promoting learning; sixth, job-related subjects were introduced such as hotel and food services and micro-electronics; seventh, connections were made with employers in providing work experience. TVEI was not itself a qualification, but it provided the framework in which qualifications might be introduced such as the CPVE and NVQ.

Such broader vision of education was captured in the Royal Society of Arts *Declaration of Capability* (RSA, 1980).

> There exists in its own right a culture which is concerned with doing and making and organising and the creative arts. This culture emphasises the day to day management of affairs, the formulation and solution of problems, and the design, manufacture and marketing of goods and services.

Reform of national qualifications

Partly in response to this academic/vocational divide, the Waddell Commission produced (1978) a major report on the reform of school examinations, the major result being the introduction in 1984 of the *General Certificate of Secondary Education* (GCSE), which brought together in one system GCE and CSE and which could be taken at Ordinary Level and Advanced Level. Its continuing success over several decades reflected the need, in major changes, for thorough deliberation by independent representatives of relevant and professional groups (including the teachers), based on research, as indeed was the case with the Waddell Commission. The National Curriculum in 1986 further enforced the need for a single system of national qualifications at age 16 which would be provided by the new GCSE, with its ten 'Foundation Subjects' (namely, three 'core subjects' of Maths, English and Science, plus Modern Foreign Language, Technology, History, Geography, Art, Music and Physical Education). It was to be overseen by a Schools Examination and Assessment Council (SEAC), thereby giving increasing influence over subject content, on which pupils were to be assessed, to the Secretaries of State (who rarely lasted for more than two years). The Conservative Party Manifesto (1987), declared

> It is vital to ensure that all pupils between the ages of 5 to 16 study a basic range of [core] subjects – including Maths, English and Science. In each of these basic subjects, syllabuses will be published and attainment levels set so that the progress of pupils can be assessed at around ages seven, eleven and fourteen, and in preparation for GCSE at 16.

Precise attainment targets would be set at each age-level in the 'core subjects' so that progress might be measured for each pupil and indeed for each school as a whole. By 1990, there would be records of achievement for each pupil.

However, well-rehearsed criticisms (fully summarised in Lawton and Chitty, 1988) were expressed because of the failure to see where central moral and social issues relating to the 20th century, or the vocational and practical studies pioneered under the aegis of the FEU and the Manpower Services Commission (MSC), or an emphasis on 'personal development', would find their places. Might it not be that significant aspects in the educational preparation of teenagers, who were about to enter society, were being sacrificed to tightly defined attainment targets through such a division of learning for all, which was defined elsewhere, which was placed within logically distinct subject boundaries, and which was ignoring so much professional thinking by teachers directed at personal and social development and pioneered under the aegis of TVEI?

The reforms of the system of qualifications entered into a bureaucratic nightmare in order to ensure the academic value of the emerging examination system. A *National Qualifications Framework* (NQF) was introduced in 1990, defining eight levels from 'secondary school entry' to 'university post-graduate' courses, and covering therefore what were seen to be the essential subjects within the new National Curriculum at different levels of attainment. It was succeeded in 2010 by the *Qualifications Credit Framework* (QCF), and that in 2015 by the *Regulations Credit Framework* (RQF). However, there had grown a range of vocational and pre-vocational qualifications which needed to be fitted into such a Framework, for example, *Certificate of Pre-Vocational Education* (CPVE) and *Diploma of Vocational Education* (DoVE). Therefore, the QCF sought to show how the many different vocational and prevocational qualifications might relate to the academic ones (GCSEs and A Levels) in terms of equivalent standards.

One major area of disquiet (which would lead to further development of qualifications and which would be complicated because of attempts to create 'equivalences' between different qualifications) was still the failure to take seriously the vocational aspirations and practical learning attainments of young people, which were beginning, as we saw in Chapters 3 and 4, to flourish in the late 19th and early 20th centuries. The curriculum reforms of 1988 seemed to underplay the distinctive qualities embodied within practical activities which made their own intellectual demands and at the same time were of economic importance. A rigid distinction between academic and vocational studies permeated the underlying understanding (and thus provision) of education, a distinction which mistakenly underplayed the intellectual demands and skills of practical and professional activities (as explained in Chapter 2), but which were increasingly recognised in the growing number of Technical Colleges and Civic Universities.

Such thinking needed, it had been thought, to be introduced into mainstream, and thus there had been instituted in 1993 the *General National Vocational Qualification* (GNVQ) alongside GCSE at Ordinary and Advanced Level, thereby attempting to bring together initially both general education and the vocational education of NVQ in five vocational areas.

Need for further qualification pathways – a 14–19 diploma

However, such constant change and haste had provoked the need for further reports on the future of curriculum and qualifications, namely: first, the Dearing Review published (1996), *Review of Qualifications for 16–19 Year Olds*, which sought to bring some unity to the 14–19 qualifications agenda. None the less, there was thought to be the need for a wider and more thorough review, this time by Mike Tomlinson resulting in the Tomlinson Report (2004) entitled *14–19 Curriculum and Examinations Reform* – declared in 'The Observer' (*17th October, 2004*) to represent

> the biggest shake-up of the examinations system in England in over half a century.

The Tomlinson Review, on '14–19 Reform', published in 2004, recommended an overarching *14-19 Diploma*, giving rise in 2005 to the *14–19 Education and Skills* White Paper. The Diploma would embrace all the different qualifications – academic, vocational and pre-vocational - and thereby provide 'different pathways' through secondary education beyond the age of 14. It was enthusiastically welcomed by Ed Balls, who was Secretary of State for Education at the time, and who said it 'could become the qualification of choice for young people'. But within three years, the proposal was dead, vetoed by the Prime Minister Tony Blair as too risky as a replacement of the academically respected A Level.

That Report had argued for strong elements to the GCSEs O Levels, constituting an 'Intermediate Diploma', and A Levels constituting an 'Advanced Diploma'. There would be up to 20 'lines of learning' within the Diploma framework, including, of course, the many vocationally related courses, taking account of work experience. The award of Diploma would require attainment in the core skills of literacy, numeracy and information and communications technology which were regarded as crucial for employment, as well as successful work experience. Thus eventually was being proposed a unified system of qualifications at different levels and with clear progressions, to replace the different and disconnected qualifications which had arisen in the previous 30 years.

The Secretary of State, Mr. Gove, however, rejected the proposals (DfES, 2005). The separate status of GCSE and A levels, it was thought, should not be undermined by being just part of the much larger and comprehensive system of awards. The vocational interests would be served instead by a three tier system of specialist Diplomas in fourteen occupational areas.

But it is useful to be aware of Tomlinson's response to the rejection by Mr. Gove (*quoted in* Chitty, 2004, p. 192),

> The short-sighted decision to opt for a diploma only for vocational courses – whilst keeping the existing 'gold-standard' exams – could back-fire on the Government by prolonging and reinforcing the traditional snobbery towards work-related education.

It would seem that the imaginative proposal for a *general education for all*, though respecting different talents, aspirations and economic needs, which had finally emerged from a history of curriculum and qualification reform, had been conclusively rejected.

Systems of qualifications reflect deep-down ideas about the nature of educational achievement and progress, and also the extent to which such achievement and progress need to differentiate between the talents and aspirations of different pupils. The unified 14–19 curriculum and qualifications system of the Tomlinson Report was seen by some to undermine the high academic standards associated with the self-standing A Level courses.

The meaning, let alone the validity, of equivalence between different qualifications (for example, between GCSEs and vocational qualifications) was questioned, thereby having a profound effect on the position of schools in the league tables. A philosopher friend obscurely remarked that he could not see how an apple can be seen as equivalent to a turnip, even when so defined by an all-powerful Secretary of State. But that was seen to be what employers and Universities had been asked to accept.

Arrival of the EBacc

Meanwhile, the International Baccalaureate (IBacc) continued as a beacon of light in a turbulent sea, valued by Universities internationally. Hence, there arose the suggestion that there should be an *English Baccalaureate* (EBacc) to be taken at the age of 16 consisting of six 'academic subjects' (English Language and Literature, History or Geography, Sciences, Mathematics, Foreign Language) to ensure that *all* 16 year olds left with a set of academic qualifications, thereby strengthening the position of the 'core subjects'.

Reasons for this innovation were, first, there was the concern that standards were falling through grade inflation. Too many pupils were seemingly getting Grade A (and even A*) at GCSE A Level and Grade C at O Level. Indeed, such was the concern over Grade C in English in the summer of 2012 that many students graded C had their marks down-graded, causing deep dismay amongst examinees, disbelief in schools and then legal action.

Moreover, the meaning, let alone the claimed equivalence, between different qualifications was questioned, having a profound impact on the position of schools in the league tables.

Second, as was clarified in the Secretary of State's 'Opinion Column' in the *Times* (*15th August, 2012*), there was now to be an 'uncompromising emphasis on academic excellence', which he saw to be threatened by 'the nonsense about child-centred learning' and 'the left-wing doctrine that academic excellence was somehow narrowly elitist', for 'our society has not always valued academic achievement as it should'.

Hence, there was seen to be a need for a qualification which consists of five or six 'academic subjects' which would be called English Baccalaureate Certificate (EBacc) – a group award ensuring breadth of academic achievement, as described above.

Being confined to the minimum of six subjects within the overall qualification, the EBacc would be compatible with simultaneous study for vocational options, if so minded, or with transfer at age 14 to Colleges of Further Education or to the new University Technical Colleges. Thus, in the preservation of academic excellence, there was some encouragement for a return to segregated schooling.

However, the evaluation report of EDSK (2019), *A Step Backward*, was highly critical: the percentage of GCSE students who had been entered for the EBacc subjects flat-lined to under 25% by 2013, and it detracted from the seen importance of both vocationally oriented subjects, which had been so carefully developed, and aesthetic subjects which were not included in the EBacc six. The omission of the Arts from the proposed EBacc caused vigorous protests from teachers and the world of music, art and theatre. The Tomlinson ideal, arising from a decade of debate on 14–19 curriculum and qualifications, had been rejected.

Similarly, the omission of Design and Technology from the EBacc subjects was a reflection of the failure to see the significance of this subject for developing not only the interest in the economic needs of industry (especially engineering, for example) but also the intellectual demands and qualities developed by such practical engagement, as argued in Chapters 2 and 3. To repeat the reference in Chapter 2 to Matthew Crawford's claim:

> The disappearance of tools from our common education is the first step towards a wider ignorance of the world of artefacts we inhabit.
>
> (Crawford, 2009)

Clarification of pathways through the 'shifting sands'?

It is difficult to understand the oft-bewildering changes during the decades following the Ruskin College speech without attending to the constant shift in different levels of, and relationships between, qualifications, reflected in the constantly changing list of acronyms which teachers in schools and colleges had to get to grips with, including the changing names and acronyms of the Department of Education itself, namely, 1964 DES; 1992 DfE; 1995 DfEE; 2001 DfES; 2007 DCSF; 2010 DfE; and indeed of their Curriculum and Assessment Agencies, namely: 1964, SC; 1983, SCDC and SEC; 1988, NCC and SEAC (merged into SCAA, 1993); 1990, NQF; 2007, QCF; 1992, Ofsted; 2007 QCD; 2010, OFQUAL; 2015, RQF; NAA; QCA; APU and of the organisations for maintenance of standards of qualifications, namely: 1986, NCVQ; 1993, FAS; 2007, QCF; 1990 TECs; 2010, QCDA; 1999, SATs. and of the many general qualifications GCE, CSE; 1988, GCSE; 2010 EBacc. and of the many, often transient, vocational and pre-vocational qualifications, namely: 1983, CGLI 365; 1983 CPVE; 1986 NVQ; 1991, GNVQ; 2008 DoVE.

Concluding comments

The evolution of the system of qualifications reveals conflicting understandings of the aims of education (and its appropriate provision) in serving the needs and wants of different pupils, their parents and the economic world for which those pupils are being prepared to enter. In the 19th century, of course, there was little need for public examinations for the vast majority. Those who entered apprenticeships were subject to the regular assessment by the Master Craftsman, and finally by the pro- duction of their *chef d'oeuvre*.

The first public examinations, therefore, were those set by the Oxford and Cambridge Local Examinations Board in 1873 for that minority of students from the Public Schools (and then the Endowed Grammar Schools) for entry to Oxford and Cambridge Universities. Central to such an education, leading to the examinations, was the knowledge of (or at least acquaintance with) the wisdom of the classical Greek and Latin literature. Therein lay the wisdom for the 'clerisy' – the 'guardian class' in preparation for their social role in society.

That would be perceived now as very narrow without initiation into scientific understanding and in the absence of a wider and critical understanding of society. None the less, its continuing emphasis upon 'the cultivation of the intellect' in its different forms and upon the acquaintance with the 'wisdom of the past' shaped the idea of the 'educated gentleman'. Subsequently, Greek and Latin may no lon- ger seemed important elements in general education, but there prevailed the view that through literary appreciation, the study of the humanities, and what Michael Oakeshott (1962, p. 488, sqq.) referred to as the conversation between the gen- erations of mankind, so one develops a distinctively human life – remaining influ- ential in the choice of 'core subjects' in the National Curriculum. The changing philosophical background to this ('the cultivation of the intellect') is developed in Chapter 10.

On the other hand, the development of the more industrial economy in the late 19th and the 20th centuries called for a more technical and vocationally related education and training for the working class, as described in Chapter 2, leading to technical qualifications at different and progressive levels. But such practical learning and knowledge, contrasting starkly with the classical education of the upper social class, pointed to a different kind of understanding and sense of personal well-being and dignity – and, as was noted in Chapter 2, to a powerful desire for more education which respected the dignity of the newly enfranchised working man. Such aspirations were to be reflected in the growth of qualifications leading to industry-related courses and degrees at the new Civic Universities.

Therefore, here we see two quite distinct pathways (marked initially by social class differences) gradually merging. The vocational pathways were finally acknowledged in technology-related degrees at the new Civic Universities. Vocational studies leading to recognised qualifications were offered in schools and technical colleges, connected very often to work experience in local industries. There emerged a relation between education (as in schools and in higher education), economic needs and vocational aspirations, reflected in the developing system of qualification.

However, it has not been straight forward. Despite the pioneering work of (for example) the Further Education Unit to integrate more active learning into the experience of all pupils, despite the recognition of the intellectual demands of practical engagement with problem-solving, despite the need for education in schools to be relevant to economic needs, and despite the plea of the Royal Society of Arts for recognition of a 'culture which is concerned with doing and making and organising and the creative arts', there still remained a deep divide between the 'academic' and the 'vocational', reflected in the rejection of the Tomlinson Report, *14–19 Curriculum and Qualifications*, with importance attached by the Secretary of State to the 'uncompromising emphasis on academic excellence', as that is reflected in the 'gold-standard exams' of the A Levels.

Furthermore, the translation of the qualifications (reflecting success at the different stages of the National Curriculum) into detailed assessment measures or targets, necessarily affected the nature of the teaching and learning experience, introducing a degree of superficiality rather than the intellectual excellence proclaimed.

Hence, the attempt in more recent years to bring the humanities and the vocational or work-related traditions together in the 14–19 curriculum and qualifications structure have not been successful. Do we need a more broadly conceived philosophy of the educated person?

References

Chitty, C., 2004, *Education Policy in Britain*, London: Palgrave MacMillan.

Conservative Party, 1987, *The Next Moves Forward*, London: Conservative Central Office (quoted in Lawton, D. and Chitty, C., 1988).

Crawford, M., 2009, *The Case for Working with Your Hands*, London: Viking (The Penguin Group).

Dearing Review, 1996, *Review of Qualifications for 16–19 Year Olds*, London: SCAA.

DfES, 2005, *14–19 Education and Skills*, London: HMSO.

EDSK, 2019, *A Step Backward*, London.

FEU, 1979, *A Basis for Choice*, London: HMSO.

Lawton, D. and Chitty. C., eds. 1988, *The National Curriculum*, London: Inst. of Education.

Oakeshott, M., 1962, *Rationalism in Politics*, London: Methuen.

Pring, R., 1997, 'Aims, values and the curriculum', in Tomlinson, S.

RSA, 1980, *Manifesto for Capability*, London: RSA.

Sennett, R., 2008, *The Craftsman*, London: Penguin.

Tomlinson, S., 1997, ed., *Education 14–19: Critical perspectives*, London: Athlone Press.

Tomlinson Report, 2004, *Curriculum and Qualifications*, London: HMSO.

Waddell Report, 1978, *School Examinations*, London: HMSO.

6

HIGHER EDUCATION

Its changing nature

Introduction

Accounts have been given in previous chapters of how the changing social and economic context of the country was leading to radical development in educational provision and indeed in the very nature and meaning of that educational experience. But Higher Education, consisting in England of the two Ancient Universities of Oxford and Cambridge (though joined in 1832 by the University of Durham) seemed relatively immune from radical change. John Henry Newman in 1852 spelt out *the Idea of a University* which identified those essential features.

However, the most significant 'regeneration' of the idea of 'University', reflecting the social and economic changes of the 19th century and preparing the country for the 20th, came not from the Ancient Universities but from the first secular University (University College London), and then from the new Civic Universities, seeking to meet the needs of the developing industrial scene.

First, therefore, this chapter seeks to identify what was central to Newman's 'idea of a University', spelling out the ideal of a 'liberal education' which was central to it, and which, despite quite radical social and economic changes since that time, remains relevant to our understanding of human flourishing and thus to education.

Second, however, attention needs to be given to the emergence of very different ideals in the founding of the secular University in Gower Street in the early 19th century and the Civic Universities at the very end of the 19th century, challenging that conception of 'the liberal ideal' and religious ethos, as they reflected the changing social and economic needs of society, and thereby affecting the subsequent understanding of 'University' in the 20th century.

Third, what must not be forgotten is the extension of the University mission to adults who, though not registered for degrees, would benefit from the civilising contribution of Universities to the wider community.

Fourth, the chapter examines the expansion and developing idea of University through to the Robbins Report (1963), which, given the increasing diversity of institutions in Higher Education, needed to specify what it saw to be the essential characteristics of University status in this more diverse system.

Finally, however, with yet further expansion and diversity (pioneering, for example, 'distance learning'), the question needs to be asked 'when is a University not a University? – or, with reference to Wittgenstein's *Philosophical Investigations* (1958. *p. 88*), is it a matter of

> the bewitchment of our intelligence by means of language [against which] philosophy is a constant battle?

Liberal education: the idea of a university

According to the editor's Introduction to Matthew Arnold's *Culture and Anarchy* (*p. xiii*), published in 1869,

> but for Newman's 'Idea of a University' it is likely that *Culture and Anarchy* would never have seen the light; different as the two books are in tone and in circumstances which produced them, their hearts beat as one.

'Their hearts beat as one' because of a shared view of 'liberal education', expressed in the Preface to *The Idea of a New University* (*p. ix*) as follows:

> The view taken of a University in these discourses is the following: that it is a place of teaching universal *knowledge*. This implies that its object is, on the one hand, intellectual, not moral; and on the other, that it is the diffusion and extension of knowledge rather than the advancement.

Therefore, a primary purpose, unlike that of Universities today, was one, not of discovery or of research (there were special institutions established for that purpose such as the Royal Society or the Royal Academy of the Fine Arts), but rather of the 'cultivation of the intellect' very broadly conceived, that is, bringing together in our understanding of the world and of humanity the different traditions of knowledge and understanding that are available and relevant, including the long tradition of ethical deliberation in moral philosophy and in theological scholarship. Focus on one or a few areas of knowledge, to the exclusion of other perspectives, would provide a distorted understanding of problems or issues. The cultivation of the intellect, therefore, lies in a broad understanding of, and in an interaction between, the particular areas of scholarship. At the level of the empirical sciences, such an engagement would reveal how limited is an understanding of a problem when seen from a one-subject perspective. For example, one would get a narrow and distorted understanding of 'persons' if viewed simply from the perspective of physiology or economics or theology. That cultivation of the intellect requires an openness to the different perspectives and a 'conversation' between members of the educational community.

Such an engagement within the University community would be driven by the search for truth rather than for human reward or economic betterment, whilst at the same time being aware that one never fully attains it. A position reached is always open to development or change through fresh discoveries or contrary evidence or new arguments.

The above account is, of course, this author's inadequate attempt to distil the essence of Newman's 'cultivation of the intellect' in his 'idea of the University', reflected too in Arnold's *Culture and Anarchy*. It is summed up in *The Idea of a New University* (p. 50) as follows.

> All knowledge forms one whole because its subject matter is one, for the universe in its length and breadth is so intimately knit together, that we cannot separate off portion from portion, and operation from operation, except by a mental abstraction.

One further observation needs to be made. The title of the book was *The Idea of a <u>New</u> University*. The context, in which it was written, was Newman's response to the invitation to develop a Catholic University in Dublin, when the opposition would be that, for the University to be an offshoot of the Catholic Church, then the idea of this being a cultivation of the intelligence so conceived would be very one-sided. The response to this, however, was that the University would not be a vehicle for religious training, or for promoting particular beliefs. Rather, however, would it ensure the study of theology (too often neglected in the secular institutions) as a significant contribution to 'the one whole … which all knowledge forms'. Theology was seen to offer an historically rich voice in the 'conversations between the generations' with both its strong philosophical tradition partly rooted in the writings of Aristotle (with the latter's delineation, for example, of the different kinds of causal explanation) and their practical significance of how the world and human nature have come to be understood through centuries of debate. Indeed, so it was argued, theology provides an alternative account of 'the whole' to that provided by a purely secular picture and set of assumptions which too often prevail. Professors advocating or presupposing a thoroughgoing materialism would, in Newman's view, be

> betraying a want of philosophical depth, and an ignorance of what an University teaching ought to be. He was no longer a teacher of liberal knowledge, but a narrow-minded bigot.
>
> (p. 58)

Therefore, just as crucial to the liberal teaching of an institution, which calls itself a University, must be theological scholarship and its claim to contribute to the search for the truth.

None the less, even within the centres of such 'liberal education' it was felt that a broader concept than what prevailed was necessary. Therefore, a Royal Commission was called in 1850, within two years of Newman's publication, to examine the growing concern that the Universities, especially Oxford, needed to embrace more fully the rapid developments then occurring in the sciences – reflected in Mark Pattison's *Memoirs of an Oxford Don*, p. 123.

From the moment [1845] dates the regeneration of the University. Our thoughts reverted to their proper channel, that of work we had to do … We were startled when we came to reflect that the vast domain of physical science had been hitherto wholly excluded from our programme. The great discoveries of the last half century in chemistry, physiology, etc., were not even known by report to any of us.

The Royal Commission led to the Oxford University Act of 1854, and the Cambridge University Act of 1856, despite opposition from within the Universities which were jealous of their independence as custodians of 'liberal learning'. Therefore, 'adaptation to the requirements of modern times' had to be part of the 'idea' of a modern university.

New universities: secular and civic

The increasingly secular influence on society, with reference in Chapter 1 to working men's labour organisations and to religious education in School Board schools, inevitably percolated through to the demand for Higher Education which would be equally secular in content and in tone. In 1826, inspired by Jeremy Bentham, University College London (UCL) was established, the first in England to be entirely secular, the first to admit students regardless of religion or none, and the first to admit women to whom degrees were first awarded in 1878. Mind you, shortly after the establishment of UCL, in 1836, in reaction to the establishment of 'that Godless institution in Gower Street', was created Kings College London, just off the Strand, and it has retained a strong Theology Faculty ever since. Both UCL and KCL later joined as different colleges in the new University of London.

Characteristic of the six Civic Universities, which were founded at the end of the 19th century or at the very beginning of the 20th, and which distinguished them sharply from the traditional Universities, was that they were concerned to reflect the scientific discoveries of recent decades, not requiring religious allegiance (for example, assent to the 39 Articles), providing 'real-world skills' often linked to medicine or engineering, and emphasising practical knowledge. They arose, therefore, particularly from the economic and social needs of the latter half of the 19th century, established by local philanthropists and industrialists who were conscious of industrial and social requirements. They often emerged from technical institutions which had prepared school-leavers for the growing industries in the northern areas of England, thus contrasting clearly with the Ancient Universities, and the social class basis of those. However, from their very beginning several of these 'red-brick universities' were open to women, whereas not until 1920 did Oxford admit women for the taking of degrees, and Cambridge even later in 1948.

The six universities were (with dates of Royal Charters in brackets):

- Liverpool University (1903), illustrating the changing conception of 'University' in response to the developing economic and industrial scene. It was originally established as the University College Liverpool in 1881, but three years later joined the Victorian Federation of Colleges based in Manchester. It was here that a professor made the world's first public radio transmission, reflecting developing interests and original work in technology of these new Universities. Useful knowledge in these areas of growing industrial employment was central. Wide communication of their discoveries was important, too; Liverpool University Press was founded in 1899.

- Manchester University (1904), developing from Owens College, which was established in 1851 by Robert Owen, a textile merchant. In 1872, it incorporated the Royal College of Medicine and Surgery, which had been founded in 1824, and including the School of Anatomy of 1814. Together with Liverpool University, there was created the Victorian Federation, from which successive northern 'civic Universities' would arise.
- Birmingham University (1900), arising from Queen's College (1825), which was the School of Medicine and Surgery, and from Mason Science College founded in 1878 by Sir Josiah Mason, a Birmingham industrialist. The Science College graduated to University College status in 1898. In sharp contrast with Newman's 'Idea of a University', the new Birmingham University established a 'commerce faculty' within eleven years of its foundation.
- Sheffield University (1905), merging Sheffield University College (founded in 1897), but itself in turn coming out of Sheffield Medical School (founded in 1828), Firth College (founded in1879, itself arising from the Cambridge University Extension Movement Scheme) and Sheffield Technical School, established in 1884 to meet local concerns about the need for technical training, especially in steel-making. Indeed, steel workers, coal miners, factory workers and citizens donated over £50.000 to help found the University.
- Leeds University (1904) emerging from Yorkshire College of Science (1874), and Leeds School of Medicine (1831). As with the other Civic Universities, arising from their origin in local or regional Colleges, so Leeds too would aim at local young people and would not be residential.
- Bristol University (1909), created from Bristol University College (founded in 1876) and incorporating Bristol Medical School in 1893, developed from the Merchant Venture Technical College, which specialised in engineering. Its foundation was supported financially by the local employers, who wanted the new University to provide for the local community. By 1924 it was providing Extra Mural courses for adults.

Thus, within the period of nine years there were established six Civic Universities. In each case they emerged from institutions which had been primarily connected with technology, textiles, science or medicine (in Sheffield, for example, serving the growing steel industry) which themselves doubtless benefited from the development of technical schools arising in late 19th century, referred to in Chapter 2. Unlike in the traditional Universities, there was strong sense of purpose to serve local communities both young people and adults through extra-mural studies (see Silver, H., 1999).

University extension: adult education

The roots of adult education, especially as supported by Universities and being eventually recognised as part of their educational mission, cannot be ignored. Chapter 1 recorded how the growing movement amongst working men for education – for the opportunity 'to learn and to think' - applied not only to their children but to themselves. This was reflected early in the 19th century in the Mechanics Institutes and later in the Working Men's Club and Institute Union launched in 1862. Towards the end of the century such clubs were instigating serious educational programmes. B.T. Hall, in a book published in 1912 entitled *Our Fifty Years*, wrote

> These clubs [by 1884, as many as 557] may become in time schools where half a million adults learn how best to take part in the great evolution which the next generation or two will witness.
>
> (see Simon, 1965, p.74)

There were several ways in which these clubs and other movements pursued their educational objectives, but in particular reference should be made to the establishment of Toynbee Hall in London's East End in 1884 by Canon Barnett, much influenced by the Idealist educational philosophy of Carlyle and Ruskin and of those at Oxford's Balliol College such as Benjamin Jowett and T, H. Green. Indeed, Canon Barnett was invited to Oxford to preach in the College Halls, from which emerged the first Settlement of University people in the East End of London. Links between these working class advocates for greater educational opportunities, on the one hand, and Oxford and then Cambridge Universities, on the other, gradually emerged, such that the University Extension Movement had by the 1890s as many as 60.000 students attending its classes (*according to the 1895 Bryce Commission*).

Despite the class-exclusiveness of both Oxford and Cambridge Universities, they, therefore, did respond to the pressure from the working class movements (referred to in Chapter 1) to provide the benefits of their liberal education. At Oxford University, adult extension education began in 1847 and, under the leadership of Michael Sadler, Student of Christ Church, had reached over 2000 by 1890 (see Hibbert, 1988, p.136). In 1888, residential summer schools had been introduced. In 1908 there was even published a report entitled *Oxford and the Working Classes* which marked the development of the Workers Educational Association (WEA) from the adult education classes. Eventually in 1947 they were united under the management of the Delegacy for Extra-Mural Studies. It is also the case that these and other classes were open to the middle classes and to women, who had not had the opportunity to benefit from Higher Education.

Subsequently the 'University Extension Movement' developed in several of the newly established Civic Universities, as part of their commitment to the wider populations in providing for them both general and vocational education. Indeed, they saw themselves, unlike the Ancient Universities, first and foremost to serve their regional communities and industries.

Such 'University Extension' soon became dominated rather by the middle rather than the working classes, which had originally inspired its beginning. None the less, the ideal of the 'University' serving the wider public, not just University members and those of a very limited social class, remained. Indeed, most Universities now have the equivalent of extra-mural departments to which members of the public can sign up. Here we see clearly (back to McCulloch's introductory statement in this book's Introduction)

> the interplay past and present has … when dealing with education,

but also we see how the understanding of the 'educated person' changes with changing social and economic circumstances.

Developing idea of 'university', leading to the Robbins review

In 1946, the Barlow Committee, concerned about the need to increase scientific manpower, urged the doubling of the number of young people entering University. Five existing University Colleges were elevated (namely, Nottingham, Exeter, Southampton, Hull and Leicester). Anticipating the promise of the Robbins Report, nearly 20 year later, the Barlow Committee declared

> No young person of requisite ability should be prevented by financial considerations from participating in these increased facilities for university education.

We noted, particularly in Chapters 2 and 3, the increasing demand in the developing Secondary and Technical Schools and in Technical Colleges for the more practical engagement and intelligence to be part of the educational vision. This was reflected in the 'ladder of vocational qualifications' eventually leading up to degree level work in the Colleges of Advanced Technology (CATs) - although such degree level work could also be pursued at certain Regional Colleges, validated for 'external degrees' of the University of London.

Colleges of Advanced Technology were established first in 1956 following the White Paper *Technical Education*. In 1966, ten CATs received the previously unrecognised status of Technological University, following the recommendations of the Robbins Report in1963 (two becoming incorporated into existing Universities). Also emerging from the Technical Colleges were other Tertiary institutions, referred to as Polytechnics (though some having their roots in the 19th Century), offering Higher Diplomas and then undergraduate and post-graduate degrees, benefitting from external validation by existing Universities especially London, and focused particularly on Science, Technology and Engineering. Following the 1992 Further and Higher Education Act, as many as 32 of the Polytechnics were designated Universities (including one each for Wales, Scotland and Northern Ireland, and two others being integrated into existing Universities).

Universities, therefore, were becoming rather different places from those envisaged in Newman's *Idea of a New University*, namely, a community of scholars in a world set apart for the pursuit of learning *for its own sake*, where the next generation could be introduced to the 'conversation between the generations of mankind' and in which the learners come to appreciate the 'different voices' of poetry, of philosophy, of science, of history which constitute that conversation. Such a University had not been seen as a place to train for a specific role or profession. Indeed, as John Stuart Mill (1867) had argued in his Inaugural Lecture at the University of St Andrews,

> There is tolerably general agreement [that a University is not] a place of professional education ... not to make skilful lawyers, or physicians, or engineers, but capable and cultivated human beings.

However, the new Universities, by contrast, had the mission to serve the industrialised economy within a tradition of advanced technological teaching, training and research. Such a transformation was one of the reforms to be recognised by the Robbins Report.

Therefore, the Robbins Report (1963) needed to clarify, in this expanding provision of Higher Education, what would count as a University and what should be introduced into the University fold from amongst the increasing number of institutions engaged in higher level work. There were three categories of such institution to consider: namely,

- Existing Universities (many of which had been recognised relatively recently): Oxford and Cambridge, London (UCL, KCL and Bedford College for Women), eight older Civic and eight younger Civic, one University in Wales and three in Scotland;
- Teacher Training Colleges (to be eventually renamed 'Colleges of Education') - as many as 146 in 1956 (a large number being very small indeed), 98 of which were under LEA control. Trainee teachers represented a quarter of all students in Higher Education
- Institutions of Technology, validated by the National Council for Technological Awards, including four-year 'sandwich courses'. Four fifths of the students, who were studying for the Diploma in Technology, attended the Colleges of Advanced Technology.

A major aim of the Robbins Committee was to create a system (with common principles) from such a diverse number of institutions, which despite their diversity, could be seen as worthy of 'University status' and thus allowed to award their own degrees, knowing that the degrees of each would be comparable in value to the degrees elsewhere. Therefore, each

- would be self-governing,
- provide a range of degree-level courses of a least three years,

- foster intellectual excellence,
- support their teaching with traditions of research,
- contribute to the general and economic welfare of society,
- have independent academic advisory committees,
- be assured of that independence and high standards by a Governing Body.

The Governing Bodies were to have a lay majority and also strong academic representatives to ensure academic freedom and equal academic awards for similar performances across Universities. The overall 'system' would come under University Grants Committee (UGC), not only protecting academic independence, but itself independent of Government influence. UGC would be the body to agree to University status of new applicants, having been assured that the required criteria, as given above, were met.

Raising Teacher Training Colleges to status of University required considerable changes to this preparation for the teaching profession. First, was the considerable reduction of the number of institutions, many becoming Colleges within the newly created University Schools of Education (one being University of London Institute of Education embracing most Colleges within the London area). Second, the professional course would be extended to four years to include both professional training and academic background leading to the new B.Ed. degree.

By 1962, when the Robbins Committee was completing its deliberations, 8.5% of the relevant age-group were thereby in full-time Higher Education: 4% in Universities, 2.5% in the Colleges of Education, and 2% in Further Education Institutions. But the educational experience of most was far removed from that of the privileged few who attended University in the 19th Century, reflecting very different economic and social conditions. To what extent could Newman's 'Idea' still be seen as valid?

Grounds for concern?

In so many respects, the idea of a 'liberal education', as developed in Newman's *Idea of a University* and as sustained by subsequent influential writers such as Matthew Arnold and Michael Oakeshott, has been preserved in the minds of many and in the educational vision of institutions and University teachers. It remains an ideal against which the educational character of Universities within the rapidly developing system might be appraised. However, the extremely large expansion of the 'system' of Universities in the last three decades would suggest how that vision has been both expanded, yet at the same time possibly undermined.

There would be two areas of concern with the development of the University system during the years following the Robbins Report.

The first would be what seemed to be the changing concept of University. The objections raised by John Stuart Mill, reflected in the quotation above, would continue to question the changing educational mission and essence of the University.

How far is Newman's 'Idea' compatible with its emerging purpose, following the expansion from former Technological and Teacher Training Colleges, as expressed by the 1997 National Committee of Inquiry (1997), *Higher Education in a Learning Society*? Emphasis was being given to the economic purposes of the University, providing appropriate 'manpower' for national and local industries and businesses, and equipping students for the world of work. 'Education' came increasingly to be seen as an 'investment' on which there would be 'returns' for both the students and business. In 1995, the Prime Minister, Mr. Major, affirmed his belief in the close connection between economic and educational purposes by amalgamating two ministries, appointing a Minister of Education and Employment, and subsequently seeking to found a University for Industry ('creating a national learning framework'). As Maskell, D. and Robinson, I. (2002, p.4) indicate (quoting from F.R. Leavis' *Education and the University*), such a neglect of the University tradition of liberal learning could be saved

> from being *explicitly* enemies of liberal education only by their 'completeness of unconsciousness' that there has ever been any such thing in the world.

Such a 'completeness of unconsciousness' was reflected in, and reinforced by, the changed language of education, especially that of 'measurement' and 'targets' - a matter to be explored further in Part II of this book.

By contrast, however, it was argued in the Newbolt Report of 1921, that

> the 'red-brick', provincial Universities were founded, as outposts of the spirit of Oxford and Cambridge, ... for instance: the rise of modern Universities has accredited an ambassador of poetry to every important capital of industrialisation in the country.
>
> (Maskell and Robinson, ditto, p.4)

Could it not be the case, first, that the development of technological understanding might be enhanced within a broader cultivation of the intellect, one indeed assisted by an aesthetic appreciation as argued by such Idealist philosophers as William Morris, Matthew Arnold, F. D. Maurice, and H. Tawney, as referred to in Chapter 2? Oakeshott's conversation between the generations of mankind (Oakeshott, 1962, *pp. 488 sq.*), though no longer 'in a place set apart', would be both possible and desirable within a context more focused on the much-changed economic and industrial context.

Could it not be the case also that just as the idea of an 'educated person' would now include not only an initiation into the humanities (the 'cultivation of the intellect' as once conceived) but also into an understanding of the technological basis of the society in which one lives and of the facilities upon which one depends?

Several of the new universities, formerly polytechnics or higher level technical colleges (for example, Middlesex Metropolitan University) had created degree courses in close conjunction with local employers such that there was an interconnection between theoretical development and practical engagement with the technological concerns of the employers and local society. There was dialogue in the formation of courses, in practical implementation through work experience and in employer involvement in the teaching. Could this not be an extension of the liberal ideal of the 'cultivation of the intellect' in a very different society from that of Newman's?

The second area of concern with the development of the University system lay in its rapid extension and its increasing dependence therefore on attracting sufficient students to make each University viable, even when the economy was not so prosperous and when competition between institutions for students necessarily affected the nature and the quality of teaching and of research traditions allied to such teaching. Gone, it would seem, would be many of the safeguards to ensure the standards and qualities expected of Universities. As Hudson and Mansfield argued in the Foreword to their book *Universities at the Crossroad*,

> one of the challenges of U.K. Higher Education today is that in some regards the sector as a whole is fragmenting as its individual institutions need to be increasingly commercial and act more competitively within working funding constraints.

Concern therefore was expressed at the low quality of some degrees and at grade inflation. As reported in *The Guardian* (*12.1.18*), the percentage of graduates with 1st Class degrees rose to 26% in 2016/17 from only 18% in 2012-13. Concern also was expressed by OfS (Office for Students, as reported in *The Guardian 25.1.19*) at the number of unconditional offers of places on degree courses, which had arisen from 3,000 in 2013 to 117,000 in 2018, and subsequently 'unconditional conditional offers', in order to maintain a viable number of students in a 'competitive market'. Inflation of costs had outpaced income and the Augar Review in 2020 proposed freezing the current 'student resource' until 2022/23, anticipating a 11% drop in real terms.

It would seem to be the case that the 'liberal ideal' had been rightly expanded to embrace the scientific and technological contribution to the 'cultivation of the intellect', and to its extension to the wider public through 'external outreach', but was in danger of being undermined by too heavy a focus on economic utility and market competition.

The present, as has been described, was presenting a very different social and economic context from that which existed in the time of Newman. Schools, as we have seen in Chapter 5, had become very different places. So, too, were Universities adapting in response to the social and economic changes and needs. The question then arises as to how far such changes can take place before the word 'university' comes to be used purely equivocally. New institutions of Higher Education might trade on the name and thereby reputation of 'University' whilst denying certain features which should be of their essence, and indeed emphasised in the Robbins Report.

Concluding comment: into 20th century – a changing concept?

Newman's idea of the University as a place *set apart* for the cultivation of the intellect (requiring, according to Coleridge, 1830, a specially educated group of people, namely, 'a clerisy'), and dedicated to the extension and diffusion of knowledge, not to its advancement, was put forward as a recipe (so influencing Matthew Arnold)

> for the harmonious development of those qualities and faculties that charac-
> terise our humanity.
>
> (Arnold, 1869/1963, p.x)

In pursuing that essentially teaching mission, the University so conceived was not a centre for discovering new knowledge ('research centres' in present-day parlance), because 'to discover and to teach are distinct functions' (*p.xiii*). Indeed, 'the great discoveries in chemistry and electricity were not made in Universities' (*p.xiv*). Nor was it a place for producing useful knowledge. Indeed, Newman dismissed the charge which was made against his view of liberal education, and indeed supporting

> their remoteness from the occupations and duties of life… in other words, their *inutility*.
>
> (p.2)

Such an acceptance of 'inutility' provided a sharp contrast with both the function and the origins of the new Civic Universities which were to help shape education in the 20th century, first, because the prevailing concept of liberal education contained an implicit criticism of the view that practical engagement would provide a distinctive insight into knowledge and its advancement. But, as argued in Chapter 2 of this book, there is a distinctive 'knowing how', not reducible to 'knowing that', which is an essential element in apprenticeship training, and which would likewise be the case in the pursuit and understanding of theoretical advances. For example, the incorporation of medical schools within five of the six Civic Universities referred to above brought together the integration of practical and growing theoretical knowledge. From the beginning each of the new universities found a central place for technology of various kinds, thereby advancing knowledge in serving the local industrial developments in steel-producing, electronics and textiles.

However, a second mark of a sharp contrast between the Ancient and the new Civic Universities, would be that the latter, unlike the traditional ones, owed, as we have seen, much to the initiatives and sponsorship of local business people, whose motives lay both in the needs of their industries and in a philanthropic desire to help their communities, not in the cultivation of the intellect for its own sake for a superior class of people.

Therefore, arising from the 19th century, and helping to reshape what one means by 'education' and its purposes for the 20th century, was, one might say, a developing concept of Higher Education, but recognisable within a continuing tradition of 'liberal education'. Such a concept is developed further in the recent book by Professor John Sullivan, 2018, *The Christian Academic in Higher Education: the consecration of learning*, in which the nature and ethos of University institutions is addressed as places not simply for the isolated delivery of specific areas of knowledge but where there is fostered a spirit of academic fellowship amongst the lecturers, a friendship based... on a shared pursuit of wisdom'.

(p. 135)

for the pursuit of truth has the character of being 'an infinitely demanding, never yet attained ideal' which puts a high premium on intellectual exchange, cognitive challenge and conceptual understanding'. And in the light of such knowledge and broader traditions (including religious and spiritual), students are enabled to look more deeply into their personal lifestyles and the sort of life worth living.

It is important to ask how far this distinctive ideal of the University may (or can) survive the very different pattern of 'distance learning', very much pioneered by the Open University in Britain through the course material carefully monitored by external advisers and by the increasingly sophisticated interactions between students and tutors made possible through advanced technology. The current closures of Universities, arising from the coronavirus pandemic, has opened up different modes of teaching and learning.

However, more significantly in recent developments has been the birth of the 'managed university', with a very different sort of ethos, reflected in the Jarratt Report of 1985 which was coterminous with 'public service reforms'. These introduced a language which would have been alien to Newman, Oakeshott and Mill, and via which reality is conceptualised so very differently such that we may be wise to heed Wittgenstein's warning (1965, p.68) against being 'bewitched by the misuse of words' in a case of 'language going on holiday'. According to the Jarrett Report (1985):

> The crucial issue is how a University achieves the maximum value for money consistent with its objectives (2.12). Each department should maintain a profile of 'indicators of performance' to include standing costs of space, utilities (telephones, etc.), market share of applications, class sizes, staff workloads, graduation rates and classes of degrees (3.33). A range of performance indicators should be developed, covering both inputs and outputs and designed for use both within individual Universities and for making comparisons between institutions (5.4). The headships of departments... ideally should be both a manager and a leader.
>
> (4.27)

In 2017, the Office for Students (OfS) was created, taking over from the Higher Education Funding Council as the main regulator for Higher Education and sponsored by the Department of Education, under the Directorship of Sir Michael Barber, founder and chairman of the Delivery Association, once in charge of Prime Minister Blair's 'Delivery Unit', and, being the master of the science of 'deliverology', adviser to governments worldwide on the delivery of improved outcomes.

We need to ask 'When is a university not a university?', and whether it is a case of

assimilating the description of the uses of words in this way cannot make the uses themselves any more like one another. For as we see, they are absolutely unlike.

(Wittgenstein, 1958, p. 10)

References

Arnold, M., 1869/1963, *Culture and Anarchy*, Cambridge University Press.
Augur Report, 2019, *Review of Post-18 Education and Funding*, London: HMSO.
Barlow Committee Report, 1946, Scientific Manpower, *Cmd* 6824.
Bryce Commission, 1895, *Report of the Royal Commission on Secondary Education*.
Coleridge, S.T., 1830, *The Constitution of Church and State*, London: Dent and Sons.
Dearing Report, 1997, *Higher Education in the Learning Society*, London: HMSO.
Firth, I.D'E. (1949), *Winchester College*, London: Winchester College Publications.
Hall, B.T., 1912, *Our Fifty Years*, (referred to in Simon, 1965, pp. 73–75).
Hibbert, C., editor, 1988, *The Encyclopaedia of Oxford*, London: Macmillan.
Hudson, L. and Mansfield, I. *Universities at the Crossroads*, London: Policy Exchange.
Jarratt Report, 1985. *Enquiry into Higher Education*, London: HMSO.
Leavis, F.R., 1948, *Education and the University*, London: Chatto and Windus.
Maskell, D. and Robinson, I., 2002, *The New Idea of a University*, Thorverton, Exeter: Imprint Academic.
Mill, J.S., 1867, 'Inaugural Lecture', Cavanagh, F.A. (ed.) 1931, *James and John Stuart Mill on Education*, Cambridge University Press.
National Committee of Inquiry into Higher Education, 1997, *Education in a Learning Society*, London: HMSO.
Newman, J.H., 1852/1919, *The Idea of a New University*, London: Longman, Green and Co.
Newbolt Report, 1921, *The Teaching of English in England*, London: HMSO.
Pattison, M. *Memoirs of an Oxford Don*.
Robbins Report, 1963, Higher Education: Report of the Commission on Higher Education, Cmnd 2165.
Royal Commission, 1853, *Universities of Oxford and Cambridge*.
Silver, H., 1999, *Journal of History of Education Journal*, 28(2) No. 173.
Simon, B., 1965, *Education and the Labour Movement*, London: Simon and Wishart.
Sullivan, 2018, *The Christian Academic in Higher Education: The Consecration of Learning*, Palgrave Macmillan.
Wittgenstein, L., 1958, *Philosophical Investigations*, 2nd ed., Oxford: Basil Blackwell.

7

RELIGIOUS INFLUENCE

Education and Faith Schools

Introduction

A major contrast between the 19th century and the 21st century (which affects the conception of the 'educated person' and thereby of the educational development to be encouraged within the educational system) lies in the change from an all-pervading religious background to a predominantly secular one in an understanding of reality.

That religious background comes across very clearly in the very structure and ethos of the Ancient Universities of the 19th century, as it did too in the ethos of the Public Schools. This will be shown and illustrated in the following section. However, its gradual diminishment can be seen in the growing criticism by the secularists, especially as reflected in the early insistence of the Secular League (formed in 1907) that the teaching of religion was not the responsibility of the State and should not be required in non-faith schools. Indeed, the continuation of religious responsibility for schools in the continued existence of 'Faith Schools' has remained a constant point of criticism by the Humanists, who argue that such religious teaching and influence is a matter of indoctrination – the very antithesis of 'education'. For example, as Richard Dawkins argued,

> The most obvious and serious case of government-imposed religion [does not] so much teach about religion as indoctrinate in the particular religion that runs the school.
>
> (*New Statesman, 19.12.11*)

And, surely, 'indoctrination' is the very antithesis of 'education'!

A compromise was made in the 1944 Education Act, as will be explained in a further section of this chapter, but such a compromise necessarily reflects rival understandings of the 'educated person', and indeed has to meet the accusations of indoctrination which invite yet further philosophical reflection on the kind of learning which constitutes 'human flourishing' and which should be covered in the educational programme.

Therefore, the following sections will:

- revert to the accounts of both the Ancient Universities and the Public Schools to see how the religious context was integral to the educational experience and formation provided;
- reflect the shift in what Charles Taylor (2007) referred to as the 'horizons of significance', thus transforming the place of religious understanding in the 'cultivation of the intellect';
- show how such disputed territory resulted in divisions between 'religious' and 'secular' in terms of school organisation – with different understandings of educational aims;
- point to the philosophical issues which underlie claims to retain religious understanding in the idea of an 'educated person' and thereby within educational formation.

Religious basis for education in 19th century

The gradual emergence of education for all children through the Elementary School system was largely made possible, as explained in Chapter 1, by the different Churches, especially the Church of England. From 1833, grants were given for this purpose by the Government to the National Society for the Promotion of the Education of the Poor according to the Principles of the Established Church, and to British and Foreign School Society of the Dissenters. Therefore, there was a strong understanding that religious belief and allegiance were, and should be, at the core of Elementary Education as an extension of the parish community. But, even as early as that, this was by no means a unanimous feeling. As referred to in Chapter 1, an undated pamphlet of the 1850s argued for a government tax 'to raise funds for a national system of *secular* education for the people'. And we can see from Chapter 1 and subsequent chapters how there remained divisions within society over the role of religion both in the provision and in the content of education within the Elementary System of schools. However, such a division did not prevail in the education of the more privileged social classes, either at the Ancient Universities of Oxford and Cambridge or at the Public Schools.

There were but two English Universities at the beginning of the 19th Century (Oxford and Cambridge) and one Scottish (St. Andrews). They were joined in 1826 by University College London and a little later by Kings College London which, being founded by the Church of England, tried to counter the influence of 'that Godless Institution in Gower Street'. Both Oxford and Cambridge were Collegiate Universities, the oldest Colleges stretching back to the 13th Century. In most, if not all, cases the Colleges were religious foundations, preserving that religious character thereafter, although changing allegiance at the Reformation. Merton College, Oxford, for example, founded in 1274 with the Archbishop of Canterbury as its

Visitor, promoted the study of theology as well as medicine and the arts. Many of the Fellows during this early period went into the service of the Church. Similarly with Balliol College, founded at roughly the same time as Merton, with Theology and Philosophy being the main subjects of study and with many of the students and Fellows eventually appointed as Bishops. The Chapel was a central building in all the ancient Colleges with regular liturgical services, and to this day three Colleges still have Choir Schools attached to them with the sung liturgy open to the public. Many of the Fellows of the different Colleges would be ordained and would serve parishes in the vicinity, with special relations to the respective Colleges.

In his influential book, *The Idea of a New University*, John Henry Newman (a former Fellow of Oriel College Oxford) defended the idea of a Catholic University, which was proposed to be founded in Dublin. He argued on the basis of the impossibility of a purely secular and therefore non-religious education. Education should be an opening to the different cultural and intellectual ways in which we have come to appreciate the world. Religion, reflected in theological thinking, as well as in critically evolved ways of life, must be part of that 'cultivation of the intellect', which defines the distinctive purpose of the University.

Very similar was the case with the nine major 'Public Schools' of the 19th century. Winchester School, for example, was founded by the Bishop of Winchester in the 14th century. Continued loyalty to the Church remained after the Reformation, as reflected in the daily chapel services. Whether or not the College members were devout in their practising of religion, what Charles Taylor (2007) referred to as the background 'horizons of significance' were all-pervasively religious.

Changing 'horizons of significance' – secularisation of society

By 'horizons of significance' are meant the background values and beliefs, which, though not necessarily explicit, are assumed and mainly unchallenged in how one lives, makes decisions and relates to other people. They constitute the moral reference points (or lack of them) in one's thinking. In the 19th century educational provision, whether at the Ancient Universities or at the Elementary or Public Schools, such 'horizons' were unquestionably religious and reinforced through chapel, prayers, presence of clergy in positions of responsibility, and works of art. Gradually, however, as we have seen, in the words of Taylor (*p.2*),

> As we function within various spheres of activity – economic, political, cultural, educational, professional, recreational – the norms and principles we follow, the deliberations we engage in, generally do not refer to God or to any religious beliefs; the considerations we act on are internal to the 'rationality' of each sphere.

It was not until Jeremy Bentham's promotion of the new University of London in 1826 (that 'Godless Institution in Gower Street') that the 'religious horizons' were explicitly rejected within the University sector. And that shift would remain constant in the establishment of the new Civic Universities at the beginning of the 20th Century. Theology might thereafter be part of the studies for a small number of students in later establishments, but by and large religious understanding and interpretation of the world would no longer play a significant part in the 'culture of the intellect' – except in the case of higher education foundations established by religious bodies explicitly for that purpose.

Such shifting horizons are reflected, too, in the decline in religious practice. According to the British Social Attitudes Survey (*BSA, 2018*), those identifying themselves as Christian declined from 66% to 38% between 1983 and 2018 and those claiming no religion rose from 31% to 52%. Such 'shifting horizons', therefore, inevitably affected the nature of previously assumed moral commitments which had been explicitly supported by religious understandings, such as the permanence of marriage and the prohibition of same-sex relationships.

School organisation: different educational values

The call for a 'non-sectarian' education within the Elementary Schools was made by the National Education League in 1869, as explained in Chapter 1. To some extent that call was answered by the 1870 Education Act which established School Board Schools, paid for by the local rates. Church schools within the Elementary System would continue but objections were raised by the Non-conformists to there being tax-payers' money for supporting Church of England Elementary Schools within the authority of the local School Boards. There were objections, too, to the teaching of religious doctrines in the School Board schools, so that a compromise was reached by which the teaching of religion would have to be non-denominational and by which parents would have the right to withdraw their children from religious classes, should they so wish (the 'Cowper-Temple Clause').

The tension between 'education on the rates' and a religious basis for education (either institutionally or within the otherwise secular syllabuses) continued through to the 1902 and subsequent Education Acts, and not resolved until the 1944 Education Act. That Act thought it had resolved the issue by creating three kinds of school within the State system: Voluntary Aided, Voluntary Controlled and Community Schools, which had no religious affiliation. The Voluntary Aided status met the requirements of the Catholic Church, gaining a certain independence within the State system, but at a price, namely the Church having to make a major contribution to the building costs of any new schools.

The three types of school reflected different and disputed understandings of religion within education for young people, and in some respects different views of 'the educated person' to be attained. The 'horizons of significance' (to revert to that phrase) would be generally Christian, reflected in the continued teaching of 'religious education' and in the daily assembly, though that teaching of religion became increasingly an introduction to the different religions which shaped the world. The Voluntary Controlled schools under the trusteeship mainly of the Church of England would work 'within a Christian ethos', though welcoming everyone of other or of no religion. It would be characterised, for instance, by prayers at morning Assembly and the singing of hymns. The Durham Report 1970, entitled *The Fourth R*, argued for the importance of Church Schools in the national system because of the values, derived from the Christian inheritance, which were embodied in our culture and which militated against the increasing secularisation of society. The Dearing Report, 2001, *Way Ahead: Church of England Schools in the new Millennium* placed these schools at the centre of the Church of England's mission, fostering 'a spiritual dimension to the lives of young people, within the tradition of the Church of England in an increasingly secular world'. Indeed, the advocacy of a 'Christian ethos' was emphasised by the Church of England Report of 2002 in its 'offering of an enduring alternative to the growing secular values of society'.

The Voluntary Aided Schools (mainly Catholic, but also some Anglican, Jewish and Muslim) were based on the view that a religious understanding of life (for example, a sense of 'the sacred' as an alternative to secular modes of thinking and living) requires an initiation into a distinctive tradition and appreciation of experience which has been inherited from generations of historical scholarship, critical thinking and spiritual life. To repeat what was written in a defence of Faith Schools within the State system,

> The voluntary aided schools, therefore, would claim, as their *raison d'etre* within the broader system, to provide a form of education which has a distinctive narrative which illuminates our understanding of human nature and of the place of each human being within the divine order of things. The upholder of such a view would be deeply suspicious of handing the nurturing of the next generation to a political system which may have no wish to protect it, and no way of providing insight into it.
>
> (Pring, 2018, p.76)

In so saying, one is drawing upon a distinctive philosophical tradition affecting the nature and the purpose of education, and thereby affecting thousands of schools world-wide and over 1000 schools in Britain – to be explained, therefore, within a distinctive philosophical tradition in Chapter 13.

Here, therefore, we see in the educational system different underlying understandings of human development – that is, the kinds of life to be pursued based on different narratives marked by religious concepts and ethical modes of thinking. That being the case, it would seem that there are competing ideas of what constitutes an *educational* system, and thereby of what constitutes the 'educated' human being so produced. Is this not an example of McCullock's claim that (as reflected in the accounts of education in the 19th century given at the beginning of this chapter and those given subsequently) what we mean by 'education' reflects the changing economic and social changes in society?

Underlying philosophical issues

The basic philosophical question, underlying whether or not there should be a place for religious ethos and religious teaching within the provision of education, lies in the claimed rationality of such beliefs and practices. A prime aim of education would be the development of reason in its different forms, and thus the attainment of beliefs, the truth of which are based on evidence and argument. Issues of truth and falsity are central.

There is a long philosophical tradition (as explained further in Part II, Chapter 11) and argued by the British empiricist philosophers such as Hume and Locke, and represented in the latter years by A. J. Ayer (1936) in his influential book, *Language, Truth and Logic*, that only those beliefs can be demonstrated as true which are revealed to be so ultimately by reference to the evidence of the senses (seeing, hearing, feeling). All other beliefs (for example, religious) which are not so verifiable are irrational and therefore certainly not part of that 'conversation between the generations of mankind' which constitute the rational life of being human – and thus not to be an element in the educational provision leading to 'human flourishing'.

There are inevitably difficulties in such a philosophical view, most obviously that of the theory itself which is not itself open to verification but also (one should acknowledge) in the justification for moral beliefs which are not themselves open to critique by empirical evidence. However, we do in fact reason about philosophical and ethical claims, about what people are thinking or about what they mean, without such reasons finally being accepted by reference simply to what we perceive through the senses. There are different forms of discourse with their own distinctive criteria of validity, which may not lead to the 'certainty' characteristic of scientific reasoning but which are intelligible accounts of experience and which have withstood critical questioning within long-standing traditions. Thus we see in major religious traditions the development of arguments through which beliefs are clarified, evidence put forward and questioned, and conclusions tentatively reached – the 'development of doctrine' through critical enquiry by philosophers from Aristotle and Plato onwards in what Oakeshott (1962) referred to as the conversations between the generations of mankind.

Furthermore, there are experiences, through which life, its values and its purposes are interpreted and which are embodied in particular modes of life and rituals, which constitute a form of understanding and which have survived criticism. They are a living embodiment of beliefs, articulated in words, though never completely captured by them. Such are variously referred to by William James (1902) in *The Varieties of Religious Experience* and Otto (1923/1958) in the *Idea of the Holy*. As James stated

> as if there were in human consciousness a sense of reality, a feeling of objective presence, a perception of what we might call 'something there'.

And Pascal, 1670, quoted in Cottingham (2009, p.121), explains this human consciousness of there being a God

> as hidden Himself from direct human knowledge, indeed, the very name He gives Himself in Scripture is *Deus Absconditus* – the hidden God (*Isaias 45:15*) … God has appointed visible signs … to make Himself known to those who seek Him sincerely … He has nonetheless veiled these signs in such a way that He will be discerned only by those who seek Him with all their heart.

In 'Faith: meaning and reasonableness' and 'Belief in God: knowledge, belief and assent', this author elaborates on the above arguments at much greater length (Pring, R. 2020).

Conclusion

The aim of this book is that of learning from the past with a view to developing future educational policy and practice. In so doing, it aims to show how, through critical examination of different social and economic practices, which characterised the historical shaping of society, the very idea of *being educated* evolved, understandably creating different and at times competing aims of education, educational policies and educational provision.

This chapter has sought to illustrate this from the long-standing and yet contemporary arguments about the place of religious belief and practice in our understanding of what it means to be educated and therefore in the different arrangements which such understandings entail. In particular, it draws attention to those changing 'horizons of significance' whereby it would seem that there are necessarily fundamental disagreements between those of religious faith and those who reject such a faith and dwell within a purely secular understanding of reality. Part II of this book, in identifying more explicitly the different philosophical positions, which underlie the changing conceptions of 'education', will seek to see how far such competing visions might be reconciled in the idea of the educated person, or at least in educational provision.

References

Ayer, A. J., 1936, *Language, Truth and Logic*, London: Penguin.

Bryce Commission, 1895, *Royal Commission on Secondary Education*.

BSA, 2019, *British Social Attitudes Survey*, 2018, London: The King's Fund.

Chadwick Report, 2012, *Going for Growth: Transformation for Children, Young Persons and the Church*, London: SPCK.

Cottingham, J., 2009, *Why Believe?* London: Continuum.

Dawkins, R., 2011, New Statesman, 11 December.

Dearing Report, 2001, *The Way Ahead: Church of England Schools in the New Millennium*, London: Church House Publications.

Durham Report, 1970, *The Fourth R: Report of the Commission on Religious Education in Schools*, London: SPCK.

James, W., 1902, *Varieties of Religious Experience*, London: Gifford Lectures.

Newman, J.H., 1852, *The Idea of a New University*.

Oakeshott, M., 1962, *Rationalism in Politics*, London: Methuen.

Otto, R., 1923/1958, *The Idea of the Holy*, Oxford University Press.

Pascal, E., 1670, *Pensees*, ed. Krailsheimer, A. J., Penguin: Harmondsworth.

Pring, R., 2018, *The Future of Publicly Funded Faith Schools*, London: Routledge.

Pring, R., 2020, *Challenges for Religious Education*, London: Routledge.

Taylor, C., 2007, *A Secular Age*, Harvard University Press.

8

CHANGING POLITICAL CONTROL

Introduction

Following the 1944 Education Act, educational provision would be seen as 'a national service locally administered', in which the Minister (as was then entitled) had but two major responsibilities, namely, first, to ensure that there were enough school places for all children, and second, to ensure there were enough teachers for the schools. The Minister had no control over what was taught or how it was taught, although, in ensuring there were to be enough school places, distinctions were made between three types of secondary school, namely: grammar, technical and modern. These were to correspond to the three types of adolescent as noted by the 1943 Norwood Report, namely, those capable of abstract thought, those who were competent in technical activities and their application, and those more concerned with practical activities and the immediate environment. The 'comprehensive system' was not yet on the agenda. The system was maintained by the Local Education Authorities (LEA), financed from both central taxation and local rates, in partnership with the teaching profession, the 'voluntary bodies' (that is, the Churches responsible for Voluntary Aided and Voluntary Controlled schools), and Government. Teacher control of curriculum was something to be maintained and indeed to be fought for. There was no National Curriculum, although there were external examinations restricting what was taught in the Grammar Schools since these were required by Universities for entry.

However, certainly from the 1960s onwards, there was a gradual diminishing of the powers and authority of the teachers over what should be taught and how, followed in later decades by a shift in power from local to the central control of education by various means, including the establishment of 'quangos' (quasi-autonomous non-government organisations), which were not open to public scrutiny as were the LEAs. Such a centralisation of educational authority began to wear away at the autonomy of even the Universities.

Teachers' responsibility for curriculum

Ever since the Circular 10/65, educational thought within the secondary sector was given mainly to the transformation of the tri-partite system into a Comprehensive one, much being left to the LEAs, rather than to central Government, to arrange or not to arrange. With such re-organisation there necessarily arose questions about the school-leaving examinations where Grammar Schools pupils sat for the General Certificate of Education (GCE), but where, following the Beloe Report (1960), there was established a new examination, namely, the Certificate of Secondary Education (CSE). The CSE would be suitable for roughly half of those within the Secondary Modern Schools (or the equivalent for the 'second stream' within the growing Comprehensive Schools), the rest leaving school without any qualifications. There was inevitably much debate therefore about the validity of streaming within the new Comprehensive Schools, which often were being divided along 'tripartite lines'. More significantly was the thinking which needed to be given to a curriculum which would suit the new Certificate of Secondary Education, together with appropriate teaching approaches.

Tension, however, was likely to arise between teachers, inheriting a tradition of classroom autonomy, and Government influence as it gradually sought to raise standards. The growing influence of Government was reflected in the Parliamentary debate in 1960 when David Eccles, the Minister, expressed his intention, on what was being taught in schools, to

> try in the future to make the Ministry's own voice heard rather more often, more positively, and no doubt, sometimes more controversially.
>
> (Eccles, D. 1960)

Indeed, Government should venture into what he referred to as 'the secret garden of the curriculum'. On the other hand, the sensitivities on this matter were reflected later by Anthony Crosland shortly after his period of office, 1965–67, who declared that the only influence of the Secretary of State's impact on the internal organisation of schools and the curriculum

> is the indirect one that is exercised through HMIs. The nearer one comes to the *professional* content of education, the more indirect the Minister's influence is, and I'm sure this is right.
>
> (quoted in Kogan, 1971, p.172)

To reconcile both the wishes of Government and the sensitivities of the teaching profession, a Curriculum Study Group (CSG) was established at the Ministry of Education in 1962 with the view to thinking about the problems now confronting schools on a relevant curriculum, including appropriate studies leading to the new CSE examination. The majority of members were from the teaching profession, but membership included, too, Her Majesty's Inspectors (HMI) and representatives of the Ministry (included this author). It was chaired by the exceptional civil servant Derek Morrell. But the CSG was then succeeded after two years by the School Council for Curriculum and Examinations (SCCE), with teachers still in the majority of the 75 members Governing Council, thereby reflecting their autonomous and professional status in such matters. Indeed, the main recommendation, drafted by Derek Morrell (1966), was

> the principle that the schools should have the fullest measure of responsibility for their own work, including responsibility for their own curricula and teaching methods, which should be evolved by their own staff to meet the needs of their own pupils. We believe, however, that positive action is needed to uphold this principle.

To that end, he argued,

> Jointly, we need to define the characteristics of change… Jointly, we need to sponsor the research and development work necessary to respond to change. Jointly, we must evaluate the results of such work… Jointly we need to recognise that freedom and order can no longer be reconciled through implicit acceptance of a broadly ranging and essentially static consensus on educational aims and methods.
>
> (Morrell, 1966)

The Schools Council, therefore, produced many well researched and jointly produced working papers of high quality on curriculum development, together with Examination Bulletins (mainly concerned with the urgent needs of the new CSE). One major task was to address problems inherent in the intended raising of the school-leaving age to 16, particularly in the case of pupils 'at the bottom of the pile', who left school without qualifications. Working Paper No.11, *Society and the Young School Leaver*, engaged in an enquiry resulting in tentative suggestions for schools to consider on this matter – for example, in Working Paper No.33 (1971) *Choosing a Curriculum for the Young School Leaver*.

However, one of the most valuable contributions of the Schools Council was the development of several hundred regional centres for teachers from different schools to discuss issues which concern them and to pursue school-based research which could be widely shared. Thus, began an important tradition of 'teacher as researcher', pioneered by Laurence Stenhouse (1975) and Elliott (1991) at the University of East Anglia. Out of this stimulus for teachers to engage in research came several highly influential curriculum developments, for example, Stenhouse's *Humanities Curriculum Project* promoting ways of discussing, on the basis of evidence, contemporary social, economic and political issues.

Therefore, it was clear that, from within the Schools Council, the autonomy of the schools and of the teachers within them was accepted, but with the need for support and for co-ordinated attempts to meet the prevailing criticisms, to raise standards and to sustain the professionalism of the teaching profession.

Beginnings of government control

Criticism of standards in schools were mounting, however. The influence of the Plowden Report (1967) entitled *Children and their Primary Schools*, was accused of promoting 'child-centred teaching' – as, for example, in the much publicised case of the William Tyndale School (accounted for in the later Auld Report, 1976) which was accused of practising an extreme version of 'so-called 'child-centred education'. According to Sir Keith Joseph, in a conversation with this author, 'John Dewey was responsible for all the problems in our schools', on the understanding that this American philosopher was the great advocate of 'child-centred education'. (*The philosophical influence of Dewey's pragmatism is discussed in Chapter 12*). At the same time were published the highly critical and influential Black Papers edited by Cox and Dyson (1969/1970).

Against this increasing criticism, the Prime Minister, James Callaghan, gave his Ruskin College speech in1976. Kenneth Baker, who became Secretary of State for Education in 1986, wrote of that speech

> In 1976 James Callaghan, the Prime Minister, startled the educational world by making a speech that dared to question the quality of education being provided in many schools. Prime Ministers were not meant to do this, they should not trample in the sacred vineyard of a school's curriculum.
>
> (Baker, 2016, p. 19)

That speech was supported by *The Yellow Book*, prepared by the Minister's advisers, which set out the problems facing schools and the needs for reform, which included

> the need to make politicians and the teachers' unions realise that an essential prerequisite for effective change along lines approved by the Government was a general assault on the principle that 'no one except teachers has any right to any say in what goes on in schools'.
>
> (DES, 1976)

Bernard Donoughue, head of the newly created Downing Street Policy Unit, who helped the Prime Minister in the writing of the Ruskin speech, later said,

> In the Speech, I made sure that I included all the feelings which I shared with the Prime Minister on the need for more rigorous educational standards, for greater monitoring and accountability of teachers, for greater concentration on the basic skills of literacy and numeracy, and for giving greater priority to technical, vocational and practical education.
>
> (Donoughue, 1987, p. 111; quoted in Chitty, 2004, p. 44)

Thus emboldened, and despite opposition from the teaching profession, which saw its professional autonomy gradually eroded, the Ministry of Education, together with Her Majesty's Inspectorate, published a flurry of White Papers eventually leading to a National Curriculum. Thus, in 1977, the Ministry followed up the Prime Minister's Ruskin College speech with *Education in Schools: a consultative document*. HMI's *Aspects of Secondary Education in England: a Survey* came out in 1979, closely followed in 1980 by the DES' *A Framework for the School Curriculum*, then, in 1981, *The School Curriculum* (which suggested the percentage of time to be given to different 'core subjects'), and eventually, in 1987, *The National Curriculum 5-16: a consultative document*. The Department's *A New Training Initiative: a programme for action*, was handed over to the Manpower Services Commission, a 'quango' created in 1973 by the Department for Employment to establish and to monitor recognised standards in post-16 vocational courses. In 1990, these functions were transferred to the new Training and Enterprise Councils (TECs), there becoming approximately 50 in England and Wales and 20 in Scotland.

Therefore, it was clear that within a period of ten years much control over curriculum had passed from the professional judgment of teachers within the schools to the Ministry of Education, and then increasingly, as we shall see, to various 'quangos'. Never the less, in the years before its supersession by the Office for Standards in Education (Ofsted) in 1992, Her Majesty's Inspectorate drew upon its professional and independent expertise to make available to a wider audience (through its *Red Books* published between 1971 and 1983) proposals for the curriculum worthy of consideration, especially in terms of 'areas of experience' which should be available to all pupils' learning in a 'common curriculum'. These were: aesthetic and creative; ethical (moral); linguistic (literary); mathematical; physical; scientific, social and political (human and social), spiritual. 'Technical' was later added.

Shifting control of education through political advisers

The 1944 Education Act had established the Central Advisory Council for Education (and also such Councils for Wales and Scotland). With wide-ranging memberships of school and university teachers, local government representatives, relevant research bodies, economic and business specialists, it would be assured that educational change and development would be based on thorough deliberation and relevant evidence, free from political interference. As the Permanent Secretary of Education, John Maude, said in 1947 to the new recruit, Dr. Marjorie Reeves, founding Fellow of St. Anne's College Oxford,

> I think your final duty would be to die at the first ditch if the Government tries to get their hands on education.
>
> (Reeves, 2011, p. 187)

The Central Councils had addressed perceived problems mainly through publication of major reports, which required years of collecting evidence and deliberation, for example, the Crowther Report, 15–18 in 1959, Newsom Report *Half our Future* in 1963, Bullock Report on *Higher Education* also in 1963 (*see Chapter 6*), Plowden Report on Primary Education in 1967 (in Wales the Gittins Report also on Primary Education), and many others including those on the teaching of English *A Language for Life*, and of mathematics, *Mathematics Counts*.

However, the independent Central Council (whose Reports arose from detailed examination of evidence from representative but independent expertise) was abolished in 1986, making room for the politically chosen advisers. For example, Dominic Cummings was appointed as 'special political adviser' (SPAD) to Michael Gove when Gove was Secretary of State for Education, pursuing the promotion of Academies in place of Local Education Authority responsibility for schools. He finally re-emerged as chief adviser to the Prime Minister, Boris Johnson, in the pursuit of the promised BREXIT, and oversaw unprecedented revision to the operation of Government. Such revision included the retirement of several Permanent Secretaries of Government Departments, including in August 2020 that of Education.

The diminishing role of the LEAs

With regard to the control of schools, the responsibility of LEAs, which had been created in 1902 to ensure adequate number of well organised schools for all young people in England and Wales, was diminished with a view to transferring greater power to the 'consumers' (that is, the parents). Such a shift was anticipated in Sir Keith Joseph's 'voucher scheme' when he was Secretary of State for Education under the premiership of Margaret Thatcher – giving vouchers to parents 'to spend' on the school of their choice, thereby on the political understanding that such 'consumer power' within an 'educational market' would lead to improved standards. Those schools which failed in such a market would simply go out of business. The role of 'the market' in raising standards in State schools (and thereby a diminished role for 'educational thinking' by teachers within schools), as advocated by the Centre for Policy Studies, was influenced by the philosophers Friedman and Hayek, to whom we shall return in Chapter 12.

Therefore, following the White Paper in 1992, *Choice and Diversity*, greater opportunity for parents to choose the school for their child was seen as the key to raising standards, able if they so wished to send their children to schools which had opted out of their Local Education Authority.

At first, this led to new kinds of school, increasing the diversity of provision which such parental choice would require – namely, City Technology Colleges (CTC), Grant Maintained Schools (or 'opted out schools'), and University Technical Colleges linked to Universities (for example, Aston University Engineering Academy which eventually became Aston University). All schools would thus eventually become independent of Local Education Authorities, financed partly by Government but also (in the case of CTCs) by private sponsors and local industries which would be generously represented on the Governing Bodies. However, wealthy sponsors failed to materialise, there being eventually less than 20 CTCs. What might be regarded as the 'market philosophy' (to be examined more extensively in Chapter 11) would, it was believed, encourage greater innovation, especially in relating schools to employer needs – for example, in more work-related learning linked to neighbouring industries, as exemplified in TVEI.

The pursuit of greater independence of schools within a market-led 'educational economy' subsequently gave rise, following the 2002 Education Act, to the shift of control of many schools from LEAs to the newly created 'Academy Status', thereby extending 'market choice', but being directly answerable to the then Labour Government's Secretary of State, David Blunkett. The new City Academies were claimed by David Blunkett,

> to replace seriously failing schools ... built and managed by partnerships involving the government, voluntary, church and business sponsors ... to raise standards by breaking the cycle of underperformance and low expectations.
> (quoted in Chitty, 2004, p. 103)

The 'academies programme' was accelerated in 2010, under the Secretary of State, Michael Gove, by which time there were 273. Furthermore, several Academies would band together as 'Academy Chains', frequently under the governance of such private companies as Serco or Capita, which also had taken over other public services such as parts of the National Health and the National Probation Service. Promoters of the Academy System argued for the need to free schools from the bonds of Local Education Authorities – as though being directly accountable to the Secretary of State or to major private companies or to the management of chains of academies (which ultimately were accountable to the Secretary of State) would give greater freedom to individual schools, no longer under the control of their respective LEAs, despite the fact that any changes of status or of curriculum would have in future to be approved by the Secretary of State.

A major victim of so many changes were the Sure Start Children' Centres, supported by the LEAs. Over a thousand of them spread throughout the country on the well-researched belief that ultimate educational achievement depended on professionally staffed Centres of Learning and support for early years' nurturing and teaching, especially for those from deprived and less advantaged backgrounds. With the decline of LEAs, and the subsequent transfer of educational responsibility elsewhere, so the majority of these highly effective Centres had to close.

1988 Educational Reform Act: a national curriculum

Eventually, the key legislation, which affected profoundly, first, the control of schools and, second, what was to be taught within them, was the 1988 Educational Reform Act. The main feature of the Act was the final move to a centrally controlled National Curriculum with detailed standards of learning to be attained from ages

5–16. Progress was to be assessed at four stages, ending with the General Certificate of Secondary Education (GCSE) which had been introduced in 1986. There were to be three 'Core Subjects', namely, English, Mathematics and Science, and a further six 'Foundation Subjects' at secondary level, namely, History, Geography, Technology, Music, Art, plus a Modern Foreign Language at key stages 3 and 4, plus Welsh at those schools in Wales which were not 'Welsh-speaking'.

The assessment of performance in each subject, in each school and at each of the four levels provided data to the Government on the attainment of each school and (since it was to be made publicly available) to potential parents within the increasing marketisation of school choice. Such assessment was assisted by a further 'quango' established in 1985, namely, the Assessment of Performance Unit (APU). Furthermore, in defining success through the attainment of such assessments, it also provided the 'targets' towards which each school should strive and thus the basis for the league tables of successful and failing schools and the overall success of the new nationally controlled system of schools.

Language of management

Supporting the changed Government control of public services, including education (thereby 'to modernise those services' and 'to improve standards') was the increasing dominance of the language of management emerging in White Papers from H.M. Treasury and the Cabinet Office which sought 'public service agreements' – for example, in 1988, *Modern Public Services in Britain: investing in reform*; in 1998, *Public Services for the Future: modernisation, reform, accountability*; in 1999, *The Government's Measures of Success*; in 1999, *Modernising Government*.

What was common to these documents was the spelling out of standards in terms of overall targets which could then be 'cascaded down' to local managers or individuals of the relevant public services such as hospitals or schools. The language of targets, expressed in precise and measurable form, came to dominate judgements of success and failure. Therefore, 'teaching to the test' necessarily transformed what was implicitly understood by 'educating', as so clearly illustrated by Mansell (2007) in his book *Education by Numbers: the tyranny of testing*. He conveniently counted the amount of 'delivery language' in the 2008 White Paper (significantly entitled *21st-century schools: your child, your schools, our future; building a 21st-century schools system*), namely, 'performance' and 'performing' 121 times, 'outcomes' 55 times, 'delivery' 57 times, and 'books' only once (DCSF, 2008).

There was inevitably opposition to such language of testing. There was, for example, a 65,000 signature petition against new base-line tests, which were planned for children aged 4 and 5 in their first 6 weeks and to be tried out in September for a start in 2000, costing £10 million over 2 years to develop, then to compare results 7 years later, thereby testing the effectiveness of the school. It was designed by the NFER. But the Labour Party announced plans to scrap compulsory tests for primary school children in England (*Guardian: 17.4.19*).

The developing influence of 'management-speak' was emphasised particularly by the new word 'deliverology'. Michael Barber, responsible for 'efficient 'delivery' of policies under Mr Blair when Prime Minister, was invited to Kentucky to establish the 'Centre for Deliverology' in that State – part of the movement 'to raise standards' in the American schools. Schools were increasingly required 'to deliver' higher standards.

Such practices, and the political thinking which encouraged them, made radical assumptions about the nature of intellectual knowledge and moral understanding (that is, about the very nature of education) which were rarely made explicit and yet which in many respects affected what counts as educational success. Part II of this book, which examines the philosophical assumptions behind the historically changing policies and practices of education, attends particularly in Chapter 10 to the meaning and validity of this dominance of testing and the accompanying language in the assessment of so-called educational achievement.

Shifting control through changing qualifications

It is worth, however, to be reminded of the ever-changing attempts nationally (described in Chapter 5) to exercise this control of curriculum and of learning through the examination and qualifications systems.

Secretaries of State over the period we are considering have lasted on average about two years. Each seems to believe that the perceived problems in schools would be resolved by yet a further 'reform' of the qualifications to which teaching would be directed. A constant problem has been to respond to the 'academic/vocational divide', for example, by showing 'equivalence' between standards in different qualifications, or by including so-called academic subjects and vocational subjects in the list of those within the same and overall qualification, or by focusing particularly upon what are referred to as 'academic subjects'. Whatever the solution, however, it should depend on a broader deliberation (usually absent) over qualities and learning experiences which constitute the overall aims of education, as well as a critical clarification of 'academic' and 'vocational', (and the so-called 'fault-line' between them, a matter to be examined in Part II.

Interim concluding remarks

It was clear that within a period of ten years much control over curriculum had passed from the professional judgment of teachers within the schools to the Ministry, then Department, of Education, informed by Her Majesty's Inspectorate, and then increasingly to various 'quangos'.

Such practices (the political thinking which encouraged them and the qualifications which emerged from them) made radical assumptions about the nature of intellectual knowledge and moral understanding (that is, about the very nature of education) which were rarely made explicit and yet which in many respects affected what counts as educational success. Therefore, Part II, which examines the philosophical assumptions behind the historically changing policies and practices of education, will need to attend to:

- the political thinking and authority in which educational policy and decisions are formulated and acted upon;
- the prevailing understanding, by the political powers, of aims and standards within the vision and pursuit of 'educational achievement';
- the distinctive language through which those in political authority clarify their educational objectives, and thereby the testing of attainments in pupil and school performance.

References

Auld Report, 1976, *William Tyndale Junior and Infant Schools Public Inquiry*, London: ILEA.

Baker, K., 2016, 'The Revolution Begins', in Pring, R. and Roberts, M. (eds) *A Generation of Radical Educational Change*, London: Routledge.

Beloe Report, 1960, *Secondary Schools Examinations, Other than GCE*, London: HMSO.

Chitty, C., 2004, *Education Policy in Britain*, Basingstoke: Palgrave Macmillan.

Cox, C.B. and Dyson, A.E. (eds), 1969/1970, *Black Papers: Fight for Education; The Crisis in Education; Goodbye Mr. Short*, London: Critical Society.

DCSF, 2008, *21st Century Schools: Your Child, Your Schools, Our Future: Building a 21st Century Schools' System*, London: HMSO.

Dearing Report, 1994, *14–19*, London: HMSO.

DES, 1976, *School Education in England: Problems and Initiatives ('The Yellow Book')*, London: DES.

Donoughue, B., 1987, *Prime Minister: The Conduct of Policy Under Harold Wilson and James Callaghan*, London: Jonathan Cape.

Eccles, D., 1960, Hansard: House of Commons, vol. 620, cols. 51–52.

Elliott, J., 1991, *Action Research for Educational Change*, Milton Keynes: Open University Press.

Joseph, K., 1976, *Stranded on the Middle Ground*, London: Centre for Policy Studies.

Kogan, M., 1971, *The Politics of Education*, Harmondsworth: Penguin.

Mansell, W. (2007) *Education by Numbers: The Tyranny of Testing*, London: Politico.

Morrell, D., 1966, *Education and Change, The Annual Joseph Payne Memorial Lecture*, London: College of Preceptors.

Norwood Report, 1943, *Curriculum and Examinations in Secondary Schools*, London: HMSO.

Otto, R., 1923/1958, *Idea of the Holy*, Oxford University Press.

Plowden Report, 1967, *Children and Their Primary Schools*, London: HMSO.

Reeves, M., 2011, *Unpublished Memoirs: The Life and Thought of Marjorie Reeves (1905–2003)*, Lampeter: The Edwin Mellen Press.

Robbins Report, 1963, *Higher Education*, London: HMSO.

Stenhouse, L., 1975, *Introduction to Curriculum Development and Research*, London: Heinemann.

PART II

Prelude: philosophical assumptions and critical questions

Chapters in Part I drew on historical development of the educational system of England and Wales since early 19th century. Chapters followed the developing ideas of what was meant by 'being educated' and the different institutional arrangements, reflecting social and economic changes in society. Accompanying such developments, however, were deeper philosophical assumptions, shaping different conceptions of what it means to be educated, referred to in Part I, but not analysed in depth or treated critically. Part II identifies them more explicitly, shows how they transformed the meaning of education (often for different social groups) and examines them more critically. Therefore, there is an intertwining of 'both understandings', but concentration in Part II on that understanding provided by philosophical reflection.

The complexity of such analysis is enhanced by the often unacknowledged conflict between philosophical assumptions (even when contemporaneous) in attempts to make sense of educational aims. Jeremy Bentham's University College London, reflecting his *Utilitarian* principles, preceded Newman's *The New Idea of a University* by less than thirty years. Yet, the latter's advocacy of *Liberal Education* criticised profoundly the equation of 'education' with 'utility' by arguing for a broader 'culture of the intellect' (influencing Matthew Arnold's *Culture and Anarchy*), a strong element within the emerging espousal of *Idealism*, and in the work of Ruskin and Morris fore-fronting aesthetic appreciation as central to that 'culture'.

The ideas of *Socialism* entered the continuing debate, reflected in the paper by W.D. Morris' *On Art and Socialism*. Much later the *Pragmatism* of the American philosopher, John Dewey, provided philosophical sense (though unacknowledged) to the emphasis on the advocacy of 'practical learning' as a distinctive form of knowing, central to educational development.

The dominance of *Positivism* (reflected in the work of A. J. Ayer) supported the reduction of educational achievement to what can be measured in the language of

.red into educational management and research, before the influ-
Modernism according to which what we believe (in education as in
.1 disciplines) is but 'social construction' – the beginnings of what is now
.1e 'post-truth society'. At the same time, both *Positivism* and *Post-Modernism*
.ded the context for the subsequent dominance of *The Wisdom of the Market*,
.nich has been influential on political thinking and decision making.

However, in understanding the historical evolution through the lens of different philosophical theories, it must not be thought that such theories succeeded each other historically. Rather is it often the case, on the one hand, of rival interpretations of the same events and, on the other, of rival justifications for different practices and political decisions within the same system.

Part II, therefore, identifies key philosophical influences on the evolving understandings of education, and thereby of the developing policies and arrangements made in the light of those understandings which they generated. It is a case of the present not being fully understood without reference both to understandings of the past (in particular changes in those understandings arising from social and economic conditions) and to the underlying philosophical presuppositions.

9

SUMMARY OF CHANGING CONCEPT OF 'EDUCATION'

Introduction

Part I provided a historical account of the evolution of the educational system in Schools, Colleges and Higher Education in England and Wales, but reflecting changing understandings of the meaning and the purpose of 'education' in response both to developing economic and social conditions, and to the public and political reflection upon these. This chapter summarises eight significant aspects of these changing understandings, prior to identifying the often unacknowledged but conflicting philosophical accounts of 'educated person' (assumed by them) and of the arrangements for attaining such personal fulfilment and flourishing. Part II, therefore, seeks to make explicit such philosophical underpinnings, shedding light on what is meant by educational progression (or, 'regression', depending on one's philosophical position). Thereby, one hopes, in the words of McCulloch (see Introduction), to make 'ample opportunity to make use of the wisdom of the past'.

Changing perceptions of 'education' and its purposes

(i)   Dominance of Social Class

What comes across clearly, especially in Chapter 1, is the unquestioned division of society into distinct social classes, each demanding different and exclusive forms and provision of education, reflected in four Royal Commissions. According to *Schools Enquiry Commission* (Taunton Report, 1868), different social classes, serving different occupations, require different teaching.

For example, Public Schools and the Universities of Oxford and Cambridge were to serve the upper classes, mainly landed gentry, who would form the 'clerisy', the 'guardian class'. The formation of students would be through the classical writings and history of ancient Greece and Rome, because there would be found in

Aristotle's *Nichomachaean Ethics*, or in Cicero's advocacy of civic virtue and duty, the wisdom on which the 'clerisy' might be formed. The classical writings were resurrected by Arnold of Rugby School as the staple diet of education, developing in future leaders the intellectual ability to tackle whatever problems they had to face, through exposure to the speeches of law-givers, the role of religion, the significance and delineation of human tragedy, the civic values and the source of virtue. The belief in the superiority of education through the Classics was reflected in the contribution of Herbert Warren, president of Magdalen College Oxford, to the discussion of the Bryce Commission in 1895 on the training of teachers for Secondary Education. He argued that the student who has read the philosophical works of Plato's *Republic* and Aristotle's *Politics* has whatever theory is necessary for the practice of teaching. In addition, it would be helpful

> that a young man who has passed through an English public school, more particularly if he has been… a prefect… has had experience in keeping order and maintaining discipline… Thus the average Oxford man, more especially the classical student, ought not to require so long an additional training, either in theory or practice, as is sometimes necessary for students from elsewhere.
>
> (Warren, H., 1895)

Such an education would be fostered in the nine key Public Schools and in the Universities of Oxford and Cambridge, then much influenced by the *Idealism* of the continental philosophers Hegel and Fichte. This was fully explained by Firth one-time teacher at Winchester College, (*quoted on page 11 of Chapter 1*). Therefore, in a letter to the Clarendon Commission on the Public Schools (*see page 11 of Chapter 1*), Gladstone, shortly to become Prime Minister, advocated the retention of Classics as

> the paramount matter of education [needed for] the maintenance of aristocratic exclusiveness of a form of education which was remarkably different from that available to other classes.

This contrasts sharply with the 'education' expected of Elementary Schools, as reported in the early chapters, where the main concern initially was with the development of basic literacy and numeracy, partly because of the *Utility* of such minimum skills, increasingly so for preparation for a more demanding and industrialised economy.

(ii) Growing consciousness of the Working Class for something better
There was, however, reflected in the Interim Conclusion of Chapter 1, increasing dissatisfaction amongst the Working Class of the limited vision of 'education' available within Elementary Schools, stimulated by growing concern for the poverty to which they had been reduced. There arose Working Class organisations (for example, London Working Men's Association for Promoting National Secular Education, producing in 1836 *The Peoples' Charter*; Mechanics Institution, formed

in 1824; Amalgamated Society of Engineers; Miners' Association of Great Britain and Ireland), calling for a National System of Education, which would apply to the Working Class. Through these new *Socialist* groups, there was a

> new conception of the potentialities of living... a vision of society in which labour would be pleasurable and education the right of all men.

Such sentiments and agitation of the working class were forcefully expressed by Thomas Mann in his pamphlet of 1899.

> The demand we, as workmen, now make is for leisure, not idleness. Leisure to think, to learn, to acquire knowledge, to enjoy, to develop, in short, leisure to live ... We claim more – we yearn for culture, we demand opportunities for physical and mental development, and we openly and fearlessly declare war against all that tends to keep us riveted to the earth.

(iii) Importance of 'culture'

Matthew Arnold's *Culture and Anarchy*, published in 1869 (and much influenced, as he stated, by Newman's ideas of 'liberal education') argued for the centrality of 'culture' ('the best that has been thought and said') in the educational experience of everyone (*to be developed further in Chapter 10*). But, with the unprivileged Working Man in mind (*as stated in Chapter 2*), he asserts the importance also of 'another kind of culture', one that

> springs from the common life of the people, the culture which means cultivation of the ordinary soul of the human spirit, which sanctifies the work that men do with their hands and makes significant and beautiful the labour wherewith they earn their bread.

An important element in 'another kind of culture' was prominence given by William Morris and John Ruskin to the significance of aesthetic dimension of life but also in the economic activities of the Working Class. For Morris, in *On Art and Socialism* (1884), reform of the depersonalised society lay through making labour more pleasurable, togethe with

> dignity and satisfaction of labour to be partly gained through acquaintance with enjoyment of the arts and artistic expression.

He yearned for a 'vision of a society in which labour would be pleasurable and education the right of all', even within the very design and decoration of the workplace or factory.

Tawney, a 'spokesperson for *Socialism*', insisted upon the 'common humanity – a quality which is worth cultivation – to see all children as human beings where the spirit of equality must be expected to establish its kingdom'. Such a mode of working must respect the dignity of labour – its purpose in the grand scheme of things and the pleasure in its execution.

(iv) Recognition of practical knowledge

As shown in Chapter 2, the apprenticeship system had a long history in which practical skills, were acquired, focused on specific outcomes in, say, carpentry or metalwork, through practical engagement under careful supervision. Such skilled work had its distinctive form of knowledge – 'knowing how' rather than 'knowing that', which demanded intelligence and an understanding of underlying principles. Hence, cultivation of intellect, it came to be argued, should include practical knowledge, which Working Men had but not the classically educated Upper Class (the distinction between 'hand-worker' and 'head-worker'). Thus was questioned traditional rigid distinctions or 'fault lines' (Sennett's words) between theory and practice, between 'knowing that' and 'knowing how', which permeated the dominant idea of education and its provision. In illustrating this point, detailed reference was made to Malcolm Crawford's *The Case for Working with your Hands* and Richard Sennett's *The Craftsman* – and to the previous Secretary of State for Education, Kenneth Baker's *New Vision for Secondary Education*. Here one can profitably reflect on John Dewey's *Pragmatism* (*see Part II, Chapter 12*) as one philosophical account of the intimate connection between thinking and doing, and its implication for the classroom.

(v) Preparation for Citizenship

As pointed out in Chapter 1, F. D. Maurice, in his book *Representation and Education of the People* (1866), articulated the beliefs of the London's Working Men's College, when he argued that no so-called education would be good for the workers 'which did not recognise them as English citizens and did not aim directly at the object of qualifying them to perform their duties as citizens'. Thus was anticipated the Franchise Act of 1867, which elevated those from the skilled working class to the right to vote. By the mid-19th century, this had received strong support from *Utilitarians*, such as Bentham and John Stuart Mill, and *Idealists* such as Coleridge, Thomas Carlisle and T. H. Green. Education for citizenship became a growing theme, strongly argued for by the Spens Report of 1938 (*as shown in Chapter 3*), for there had been fears amongst the privileged classes of the granting of such citizen rights. Therefore, 'education for citizenship' – for the power and aspiration to contribute intelligently to the political shaping of society – became a significant element in the 'changing aims of education for all', both Working Class (if they were to exercise influence in the social and economic world they inhabit) and Upper Classes (if their power and influence were not thereby to be curtailed).

(vi) Relation to the changing world of work

In his Ruskin speech in 1976 (*as reported in Chapter 4*), Prime Minister Callaghan spoke of preparing future generations for life, especially the needs of industry and the technical knowledge for living in a technological society. There had been developed (following the *Royal Commission on Elementary Education* in 1888, *summarised in Chapter 1*) Higher Grade Elementary Schools and Technical Colleges.

Furthermore, between privileged upper class and working class was a growing middle-class receiving 'higher level of education' in Endowed Grammar Schools, preparing for leadership in a changing business and professional world. Further distinctions were made between three grades of Grammar Schools to meet demands of more technology-based industry.

Behind such distinctions were assumptions about the different latent abilities of the 'ruling class', the 'head-workers' and the 'hand-workers' – a three-fold classification, which persisted under different educational guises until the gradual termination of the 'tripartite system' of schools in recent years. Thus, as a prelude to the 1944 Education Act (*as described in Chapter 4*), three different types of child were seen to have different educational needs – and different destinations into employment.

(vii) Education for all? equal opportunity and common schooling
There gradually emerged the call for *Secondary Education for All* (title of Tawney's 1922 book) ever since free places were made available in 1907 for some children to proceed from Elementary to Secondary Schools. Rather did Tawney argue (*1931/38 revised edition, p. 1*)

> The purpose of the educationist is to aid [*all children's*] growth. It should be easy to regard them, not as employers or workmen, or masters and servants, or rich or poor, but merely as human beings. Here, if anywhere, the spirit of equality might be expected to establish its kingdom. Here, if anywhere, it should be possible to forget the tedious vulgarities of income and social position, in a common affection for the qualities which belong to man himself, and in a common attempt to improve them by cultivation.

Indeed, a Memorial to Bryce Commission, from the Trade Union Congress, defining Secondary Education, argued that all children should be educated in a

> 'common school' and thus realise and enjoy in their youth common interests and pursuits as the children of one country.
>
> (*Bryce Commission, vol. V*)

In this slow evolution over 150 years of the meaning and provision of 'education', there had emerged more to education than 'cultivation of the intelligence', namely, a broadening of interests and grounds for social togetherness and cooperation, namely, respect for common humanity – a quality which is worth cultivation – to see all children as human beings where the spirit of equality must be expected to establish its kingdom thereby ensuring equality of opportunity and interests across groups of young people, seeing social cohesion as a key aim, and questioning prevailing beliefs in 'fixed intelligence' and pre-determined social and employment pathways, which militated against ideals of 'equality' and 'mutual respect'.

(viii) Personal development
Throughout these social and economic developments there are the hints of a broader understanding of education than what prevailed, namely, what arises from

a conception of 'personal development', not captured entirely in the 'cultivation of the intellect'. There were references to 'human fulfilment' and 'common humanity' rather than to intellectual development recognised by formal education. For William Morris (see *On Art and Socialism*, 1884), reform of the depersonalised society lay through making labour more pleasurable, together with 'dignity and satisfaction of labour' being partly gained through acquaintance with, and enjoyment of, the arts and artistic expression.

The importance of 'personal development', in a more broadly conceived idea of 'education', comes across strongly in the experience of apprenticeship (see Chapter 4, *Further Education and Youth Service*). Examples suggest a deeper awareness of personal development through practical engagement, a sense of achievement, a feeling of usefulness and a growing understanding of the world into which the young apprentices would be entering and to which they would be able to make valued contributions. One might say that they convey a broader sense of 'personal or human flourishing'.

Much neglected, in overall understandings of educational development, is the significant contribution of the Youth Service (*developed in Chapter 4*). To repeat what was related there concerning evidence to the House of Commons Select Committee:

> Its [Youth Service] distinctive characteristics include the voluntary engagement of young people, young people's active involvement in developing provision, the use of informal education as the primary method of youth engagement and an approach to provision that is responsive to young people's preferences.
>
> (HoC, 2010:9)

Concluding comments

Many issues have been raised concerning the evolving meaning of education, and its relevance to (and provision for) different social classes, learners' abilities, and economic needs. One consequence is that more thought needs to be given to questions concerning the distinctive features of what constitutes being and developing as persons, irrespective of latent talent, social class or type of employment. This comes across in the plea of Thomas Mann, 1889,

> we yearn for culture, we demand opportunities for physical and mental development, and we openly and fearlessly declare war against all that tends to keep us riveted to the earth.

Such is implicit in the importance given by Ruskin and Morris to the aesthetic appreciation and enjoyment to be encouraged through the arts and crafts. It is there in the call for greater equality through the recognition 'of a common humanity - a quality worth cultivating', as argued by Tawney (*see Chapter 3*). That wider sense of 'human flourishing' was captured in the claim by the apprentice in Chapter 3:

classroom learning has a place but is no match for on-the-job experience – apprenticeship hasn't just boosted my career, it's changed who I am and has given me new skills, confidence and experience'.

Hence, the importance, too, in the Youth Services (*as described in Chapter 4*), which too often are the first to suffer when financial cuts are made and yet should be seen as vital in the educational and personal development of disillusioned young people.

Therefore, in the final chapter (Chapter 14), it is important (in considering the aims of education for all young people, not just the socially privileged) to focus on what more broadly constitutes this 'common humanity' and thereby 'human flourishing'.

Meanwhile, however, there is need in the next four chapters (*10 to 13 of Part II*) to examine more carefully and critically the different philosophical backgrounds to the changing concept of 'education', which have been referred to throughout the chapters and identified more explicitly in this Chapter 9, before the final chapter which focuses on the continuing theme of 'human flourishing' as the aim of education.

References

Arnold, M., 1869/1931, *Culture and Anarchy*, Cambridge University Press.

Baker, K., 2013, *A New Vision for Secondary Education*, London: Bloomsbury.

Bryce Commission, 1895, *Royal Commission on Secondary Education*, London: HMSO.

Callaghan, J., 1976, *Preparing Future Generations for Life*, Oxford: Ruskin College.

Crawford, M., 2009, *The Case for Working with Your Hands*. London: Viking (The Penguin Group).

Firth, J. D'E., 1949, *Winchester College*, London: Winchester Publication HoC (House of Commons).

Morris, W., 1884, *On Art and Socialism*, (ed. Holbrook Jackson, 1947).

Newman, J.H., 1852, *The Idea of a University*, Lectures given to the University of Dublin.

Norwood Report, 1943, *Curriculum and Examinations in Secondary Schools*, London: HMSO.

Royal Commission on Elementary Education, Newcastle Report.

Ruskin, J., 1849, *The Seven Lamps of Architecture*, London: Routledge.

Taunton Report, 1868, *Schools Enquiry Commission*.

Sennett, R., 2008, *The Craftsman*, London: Penguin.

Taunton Report, 1968, *Report of the Schools Inquiry Commission*, London: HMSO.

Tawney, 1922, *Secondary Education for All* (revised edition 1938) Hambledon: Continuum.

Tawney, R. H., 1931/38, *Equality*, George Allen and Unwin.

Warren, H., 1895, *Evidence to the Bryce Commission*, London: HMSO.

Wittgenstein, L, 1958, *Philosophical Investigations*, 2nd. Edition, Oxford: Basil Blackwell.

10

UTILITARIANISM, IDEALISM AND SOCIALISM

Introductory comments

Permeating the different debates within the 19th Century Royal Commissions (summarised in Chapter 1), or underpinning the different struggles particularly of the Working Class, were, as we have seen, notions about relevant aims of education and appropriate educational provision. Such is inevitably the case, whilst at the same time such notions may be only dimly apparent, still to be articulated, and examined critically. There would be underlying ideas about human flourishing to be cherished and about the kind of social structures and relationships which would enable that flourishing to take place. It is a job of philosophy of education, to make explicit such ideas, and to examine them critically within wider ethical and social understandings. Philosophy may help to make sense of what participants are only dimly aware of.

Philosophical influences

(i) Utilitarianism

A dominant social philosophy at the beginning of, and for much of, our period, which influenced policy and public attitudes, was that referred to as *Utilitarianism*, pursuing the 'principle of utility'. This was much in keeping with the long tradition of empiricism, arising from the 'Enlightenment', which tended to measure the value of a practice in terms of its utility. Furthermore, its utility would be judged in terms of the pleasure or happiness which the action or activity would bring about. At the public policy level, such utility would be judged in terms of the greatest amount of happiness it would generate for the greatest number. Values would generally be defined in terms of the satisfactions generated to the greatest number of people. That required assessment of the quantity of pleasure or benefit generated. One can see the influence of such assessment of value in the urge to measure effects of policy, as reflected in the introduction of 'payment by results' in the Revised Code of 1863, following recommendations of the Newcastle Commission, explained in Chapter 1.

The name most readily associated with *Utilitarianism* is that of Jeremy Bentham. As he said in his *Introduction to the Principles of Morals and Legislation* (*ch. 1, sect. 1*), 1823,

> Nature has placed mankind under the governance of two sovereign masters, pain and pleasure … They govern us in all we do, in all we say, in all we think: every effort we can make to throw off our subjection will serve but to demonstrate and confirm it. In words a man may pretend to abjure their empire, but in reality he will remain subject to it all the while.

There was, therefore, inevitably a reduced sense of the importance of tradition and of inherited values, including those arising from religious beliefs. Rather was the general principle of conduct, especially that governing social policy (which derived from such a comprehensive theory of behaviour and motivation) the 'pursuit of the greatest amount of happiness of the greatest number' – to maximise pleasure and to minimise pain within society. No one would be excluded from such a calculation, and so the privileged positions of a minority in society, enhanced by the distinctive educational institutions, would themselves need to concede such privileges.

In pursuit of such a social and moral ideal, the notion of the 'common good' inevitably arises, although its calculation would be profoundly difficult, given the diversity of pleasure-seeking activities amongst the population, and where the pleasure of one person could so easily maximise the pain of another. Consequently, there emerged within utilitarian aspirations the advocacy for some form of democracy through which difference might be reconciled, and the common good defined and pursued. These did begin to emerge with the extension of the franchise, as detailed in Chapter 1.

One prominent example of the enlargement of the 'common good' lay in the creation of a new University, in addition in England to the two Ancient Universities of Oxford and Cambridge, seen by many of the *Utilitarians* as bastions of privilege. The new University College London was founded in 1828, following strong advocacy (from men of whom Bentham was a key member) to widen opportunities for young people otherwise denied them. Bentham chaired the annual meetings, and, in pursuit of the greatest happiness of the greatest number, he bequeathed his mummified body to continue taking the chair at the annual dinner after he had died. His body still remains on display in a glass box in the University, continuing to give pleasure to subsequent generations.

However, the concept of 'the common good' had to face difficulties within the Utilitarian tradition. John Stuart Mill, a follower of Bentham, recognised in his book entitled *Utilitarianism* that there were intrinsic *qualitative* differences between pleasures, not simply measurable differences in quantity.

> It is quite compatible with the principle of utility to recognise the fact that
> some *kinds* of pleasure are more desirable and more valuable than others. It
> would be absurd that while, in estimating all other things …. the estimation
> of pleasures should be supposed to depend on quantity alone.
>
> (Mill, J.S., 1863b, p. 11)

Mill, therefore, insists that there are aspects of a distinctively human life which
need to be taken into account in deciding upon the Common Good. In another
passage in his *Dissertations and Discussions* (*quoted in* Coplestone, 1966, p. 31), he
famously asserts

> It is better to be a human being dissatisfied than a pig satisfied; better to be
> Socrates dissatisfied than a fool satisfied.

Thus we see the gradual change in the way in which *Utilitarianism* enters into
the public thinking about educational policy and provision. At first, it emphasises
the right of every one to attend Elementary School, and to gain the 'basic utility' of being able to read and write, and to have whatever skills were needed to
contribute to the increasingly competitive international economy – as witness the
Paris Exhibition (referred to in Chapter 1). Thereafter, as the franchise expanded, so
too were the Working Class increasingly becoming part of the citizenship, and that
made demands on their ability to contribute to policy discourse and thus to their
educational achievement.

Gradually, therefore, such educational needs came to recognise a qualitative
aspect of 'utility' in terms of cultural development – 'culture' becoming a key concept in the battle for education for all, related to recognising what we have in common in our distinctively human development, which (one might add in anticipation
of the onset of *Idealism*) is revealed in the initiation into a cultural world depicted by
Matthew Arnold as 'the very best which has been thought and said.'

(ii)   Idealism

One might see here the slow transition to an *Idealist* element in the understanding
of what education means for each and every one and thus what it should practically consist of. One criticism of the Utilitarian philosophical position was, as urged
by John Stuart Mill, the rather dessicated understanding of what it means to be,
and thereby to develop as, a person. Clearly this, too, would be the view of many
churchmen who were responsible for the Elementary Schools to which the majority of young children went. Religion and its significance for personal development
had been left out.

Therefore, of considerable influence was the philosopher, poet and theologian
Samuel Taylor Coleridge, who in turn was influenced by the German Idealist Hegel,
according to whom

A man's humanity is realised especially in the consciousness of his moral freedom, which enables him to give his assent to the contracted obligations imposed upon him by society.

(Barrell, J. 1830, Introduction to Coleridge, p. xii)

But that freedom, and the consciousness of it, require the education for the intelligent participation in, and contribution to, the shared interests of the community in what is referred to as the State.

Coleridge published in 1830 the influential book, *On the Constitution of the Church and State*. He was particularly critical of the narrow vision of human motivation (and, thus, so-called personal development) within the Utilitarian tradition. What was lacking was any sense of the spiritual aspect of being a person, the capability and the urge to transcend the pleasurable and useful, as that might be empirically measured, and, through a wider sense of reason, perceive *an ideal* of what it is to be human. It is interesting to note how on several occasions Coleridge refers to and quotes William Wordsworth as expressing through poetry a spiritual significance in the perception of nature. Poetry, music and art provide appreciations of a distinctively human life; they transcend the mere empirical and useful which was embedded in the Enlightenment and Utilitarian traditions. Thus Coleridge opposed the focus on vocational schemes of education, aimed solely on material improvement and usefulness. The true ends of education, the *idea* of personal development in its wider sense, were

being obscured for them … by the wrong sort of education or the lack of it, and by an economic system which converted them into engines for the manufactory of new rich men and did not include them in the ends of industry.

(Barrell, J., op. cit, p.xii)

Coleridge (1830, p. 4), therefore, showed his indebtedness to the German Idealism of Hegel and Fichte by stressing the importance of 'ideas' which shaped our perception and understanding of objects and which powerfully persisted in spite of material changes, especially in moral, religious and civic ideas. An 'idea' was

that conception of a thing, which is not abstracted from any particular state, form, or mode, in which the thing may happen to exist at this or that time; nor yet generalised from any number or succession of such forms or modes; but which is given by the knowledge of its ultimate aim.

Basically we live in a world of ideas which shape how we see the empirical world, which cannot be derived from that world, which help define how we, as persons, ought to live within that world, and which therefore help define the kind of society and political frameworks in which all persons might attain those human purposes. Education therefore lies in the gradual cultivation of this world of ideas through a range of experiences including religious, poetic, musical, and moral discourse, that is:

> the harmonious development of those qualities and faculties that characterise our humanity.

Such an inheritance is what he called 'culture' – a concept of great influence on Matthew Arnold (1869/1963), who, in his book *Culture and Anarchy*, defined such a sense of culture as

> the general harmonious expression of those gifts of thought and feeling which make the particular dignity, wealth and happiness of human nature.

For this purpose, Coleridge advocated the creation of a 'clericy' – the cultivation, at a small number of Universities, of people (particularly clergy and school teachers), who would initiate young people into such a cultural world, and who would thereby gain the wisdom to provide leadership in society at its different political levels. Links might hereby be made conceptually to the 'guardian class' of Plato's *Republic*. Such a 'clericy' would constitute a 'National Church', not to be identified with the Established Church, though much would be in common in the promotion of such an Idea.

The influence of Hegelian Idealism grew even more significant in the growing intellectual critique of the philosophical thinking of the tradition of Locke, Berkeley and Hume. The grounds for such influence lay especially in the scholarship and teaching of renowned philosophers in Oxford University, particularly Balliol College. In the middle and late 19th century, under the leadership of Benjamin Jowett, there gathered a group of Fellows and students who came to be deeply imbued with the philosophical thinking of Hegel. Most important, many of these later came to hold influential positions within the educational system and its development – for example, T. H. Green (who contributed to the Taunton Commission on the Endowed Grammar Schools), James Bryce (who later was to chair the 1895 'Bryce Commission' on Secondary Education), and Robert Morant (who became Permanent Secretary implementing the 1902 Education Act). Indeed, nearly all the forward-looking national innovations from 1870 to 1920 were brought about by former students from Balliol and connected Colleges of the University, much influenced by the introduction to the tradition of Idealism especially by T. H. Green, who had been a student and then tutor in philosophy at Balliol.

What was it then about the Idealist tradition, emanating mainly from the German philosophers Hegel and Fichte, which shaped the thinking of such people who were in positions to influence both educational thinking and indeed the transformation of educational arrangements?

Idealism, broadly conceived, understood the world, not just in the physical sense of the empiricists (that is, of a world of physical objects or indeed of atoms, related causally according to scientific explanations), but as an aspect of a world of ideas, indeed a spiritual universe, through which sense is made of that physical world. We live in a world of ideas as much as in a world of physical objects. Education, therefore, is concerned with entering into that world of ideas and into seeing its spiritual dimension, as Coleridge so strongly argued.

Inspiration amongst the Idealists was to be found in the classical philosophy of both Aristotle and especially Plato. Aristotle's metaphysics transcended, and gave deeper explanation of, the physical reality. For Plato especially, the world, in being open to the senses, was to be understood through that world of ideas in which, to varying degrees, we all participate. Education is, to use Plato's metaphor, like a path from the darkness of the cave into the light of the sun. Hence, through education we come to penetrate that world, thereby gaining insight not only into the physical universe but especially into its moral and spiritual and aesthetic dimensions. The purpose of education, therefore, would be to enable young people (the 'neophytes') to be liberated from low-level understanding and to dwell in and appreciate the world of ideas, residing (in the words of Matthew Arnold) in 'the best that has been thought and said'.

Many never manage to achieve this, and thus need to be led, if not controlled, by those who have achieved it through their superior education, who became equivalent to Plato's 'guardian class' or Coleridge's 'clericy', and who therefore should occupy positions of responsibility for the public good.

There are four aspects of this, therefore, which need to be emphasised.

The first aspect – the 'Guardian Class' – is that there was seen to be a need for educational institutions which create such a 'guardian class' – what the philosopher Samuel Taylor Coleridge, in *The Constitution of State and Church*, referred to as 'the clerisy'. These would be the teachers in the Public Schools (those such as the nine investigated by the Clarendon Commission in 1869, as detailed in Chapter 1) through which, with a particular focus on the Classics, pupils would gain that broader understanding and sense of moral purpose. Dr. Thomas Arnold, father of Matthew Arnold, was head teacher of Rugby for many years before becoming Regius Professor of Modern History at Oxford University in 1842. In his inaugural lecture he expressed the educational ideal of both the Public School and University in which

> there is, or there ought to be, something very ennobling in being connected with an establishment at once ancient and magnificent, where all about us, and all associations belonging to the objects around us should be great, splendid and elevating.
>
> (*quoted in* Sutherland, G., 1973)

Such schools, therefore, had both the capacity and the role to provide the leadership of society in the light of the informed understanding of what is a worthwhile form of life, as was argued in the Clarendon Commission (*summarised in Chapter 1*).

The second aspect – a broader idea of education for all, was that this idealist mode of thinking provided a justification for a broader idea of education for all young people, indeed a common schooling, as all needed to be developed for participation as citizens in the development of the public good and for a life in which a rich intellectual, aesthetic and moral life could be open to all. In all this there were grounds for promoting greater equality amongst all citizens, as was argued so strongly, though later, by Tawney (1938, see below). For, as Matthew Arnold argued in *Culture and Anarchy*, these values should permeate the whole nation. 'The men of culture are the true apostles of equality'. By its attachment to critical reason, its opposition to stock notions and narrow prejudices, 'culture seeks to do away with classes altogether'. (Gordon and White, 1979, p.7, quoting 'Culture and Anarchy).

The third aspect – elite schools, was, not simply the support thereby given for a broader and more enlightened sense of education for all, but also (paradoxically, given the *second aspect*) for a perceived justification for the retention of elite schools which would, especially through the promotion of the Classics at the core of the subject studied, enhance the ability and the authority of the upper social and governing class. To repeat the conclusion drawn by Brian Simon (*1965, p.318*) in reference to the Clarendon Report on the Public Schools,

> All in all, by insisting on the preservation of the classics as the main core of teaching, and by ensuring the final separation of the public schools from those for other classes, the Clarendon Commission created an efficient and entirely segregated system of education for the governing class – one that had no parallel in any other country.

The fourth aspect – the spiritual dimension to such idealist insight was emphasised emphatically by Coleridge in the aforementioned book. The poet Wordsworth, influenced by Coleridge, saw nature (like man) as an embodiment of the divine spirit:

> a presence that disturbs me with the sense of elevated thoughts; a sense sublime of something far more deeply inter-fused whose dwelling is the light of setting suns.
>
> (*Tintern Abbey*)

According to Coleridge, the State is a spiritual reality, incorporating the aspirations which the members of the State – the citizens – have in common, and mediating between man and God. That 'clerisy' would include groups of clergy to help raise this spiritual insight and motivation through education – creating a sort of 'National Church'.

Strongly influenced was F. D. Maurice who, in pursuit of the *Idealism* of Coleridge, focused not on the Public Schools as the forming of leaders, but, in 1848, on the establishment of Christian Socialism and, in 1854, the Working Men's Club in London. Influenced, too, was R. H. Tawney whose subsequent socialist classic, *Equality* (to be introduced at length below) emerged from the *idealist* conception of a society by which all are shaped, and thereby empowered to shape, in the pursuit of the public good.

As explained earlier, this developing thought, which was shaping education's purposes and political organisation for all (exemplified in the aforementioned work of Morant, Green, Bryce and Tawney) and which was manifest in the influential writings of Matthew Arnold and F. D. Maurice, was indirectly influenced by the *Idealism* of the German philosopher, Hegel.

(iii) Socialism

Chapter 1 referred to the growing consciousness of the working class of their status as citizens, resulting in the Franchise Acts of 1867 and 1884. But anticipation of such a status required thought about the kind of education which would prepare for such political responsibilities – the beginning, one might say, of 'political education'. To quote again F. D. Maurice (from his aptly entitled publication, *Representation and Education of the People*, published one year prior to the Franchise Act) that no education would be good for the workers

> which did not recognise them as English citizens and did not aim directly at the object of qualifying them to perform their duties as citizens.
>
> (Maurice, F.D., 1866)

Thus, in anticipation of the franchise, a prime aim of education within the Elementary Schools would be to introduce the children to a broader range of ideas and understandings such that they would be better able to fulfil their duties as citizens – an objective which was referred to in the *second aspect* mentioned above, and as argued by Tawney. Such would empower them through aspiration and knowledge to exercise the political power to reshape society.

Most important, however, from the political empowerment point of view, was the development of various forms of adult education – responding to the likes of Thomas Mann's pamphlet published in 1899 (*quoted in Chapter 1*).

> The demand we, as workmen, now make is for *leisure*, not idleness. Leisure to think, to learn, to acquire knowledge, to enjoy, to develop, in short, leisure to live.

This growing interest in adult education was developed in Chapter 6 of this book.

Contributing to such thinking were growing organisations of workers with what might be regarded as *socialist* ideas about society. The Trade Unions Congress was formed in 1868, but there was also a rapid development around the country of what were called 'Radical Clubs', with interest in a more secular society and the reduction of the extreme poverty of many. Many of these societies came together under the umbrella of the Social Democratic Federation (SDF) in 1884 which stood for the social ownership of the means of production, and whose early motto was

> EDUCATE- we shall need all our intelligence; AGITATE – we shall need all our enthusiasm; ORGANISE – we shall need all our force.

One such society, of lasting significance, and established at the same time as the SDF, was the Fabian Society, which through lectures throughout the country and through its many publications, focused on educating people in socialist principles. Such required the attainment of political power by the working class. The Fabian Tract, no.11, of 1891, entitled *The Workers' Political Programme* stated

> We want a national system of education, secular, compulsory and technical, at the public cost, for all classes alike.

Paradoxically enough, amongst these socialist societies, no doubt from the influence of the non-conformists and Methodists, Socialist Sunday Schools developed with their own distinctive socialist views as reflected in the one in Bristol.

> The moral truths of all faiths found their highest expression in Socialism... Socialism is a religion teaching morality and brotherhood of man as taught by Christ and others. The central principle (its god) is Love and Love of Humanity. It strives to abolish unjust laws and customs which enable the idle rich to rob the industrious poor.
>
> (Bryher, S., 1929, Pt.II, 54, quoted in Simon, 1965, p. 49)

This urge for the workers' control, argued through the many different 'secular societies' which were emerging, gave rise to a more systematically argued and philosophical understanding of *Socialism*, as developed especially in the work of William Morris (*On Art and Socialism* in 1884), and of R. H. Tawney (*Secondary Education for All* in 1922 and *Equality* in 1938). (Tawney's account of 'equality' is postponed to the Section below on Equality.)

Morris was centrally concerned with the essential dignity of each human being and with the rightful acceptance of that dignity in his or her mode of living and working. Such a mode of working must respect the dignity of labour – its purpose in the grand scheme of things and its pleasure in its execution. In this he benefited (*as argued by* Simon, 1965, p. 53) from his reading of Karl Marx in two respects: first, Marx's analysis of the division of labour and its effect on human development; second, Marx's advocacy of political revolution in order to overcome that division. With regard to the dignity of Labour, Morris (1884) looked back to the age of the craftsman who could take pride in what he was creating – the skills employed, the appearance of the finished product, the physical conditions in which he was working. There was an aesthetic dimension to his life and work (*as captured in Chapter 2*). But, in the current industrial scene, that source of pride and pleasure had disappeared in the dehumanising enslavement to machines and in the service of an exploitative class of employers. For Morris, there was a need for the workers to regain and to retain a sense of dignity in their labour, and an aesthetic dimension to their lives. For him, the role of art was essential in overcoming the squalor of work as it had become and of attaining a sense of human dignity and pleasure (*a point developed at length in Chapter 3*).

To summarise, therefore, what was (and no doubt remains) the distinctively socialist philosophical perspective to educational thinking and provision, it would be

- recognition of the equal dignity of all members of the community whatever their birth or occupation;
- need in consequence for 'education for all', that is, raising consciousness, including self-consciousness, through introduction to ideas (e.g. social, moral and aesthetic) which transcend the limited and immediate understanding of the world;
- respect for the practical knowledge and skills, too often treated as inferior in their attainment and in their occupation;
- political understanding and skills of everyone so as to become citizens within the community and thereby able to contribute to its continuing formation and policy.

As we saw in Chapters 2 and 6, such ideals necessarily extend to both apprenticeships and adult education within the socialist political framework.

Key concepts

It has been argued, therefore, that to understand the changing ideas of education in the 19th century, and to look ahead, in the light of such understanding, to what ideas, principles and understandings should be shaping the education provision in the future, three philosophical strands have been identified: *Utilitarianism, Idealism* and *Socialism*. Inevitably each such philosophical strand does not come across in any pure and unadulterated form. The *Idealists* were certainly inspired by the German philosophers, Hegel and Fichte, but that inspiration enters in different ways into the understanding of education and its purposes for Coleridge and for his successors. Similarly, with the influence of *Utilitarianism* and *Socialism*. In each case there are philosophical debates within the different traditions, compromises to be made, and different applications of the philosophical thinking to changing situations.

Therefore, here it is necessary to identify certain key concepts or ideas within and across the different philosophical traditions, bearing in mind that such concepts do themselves evolve through criticism and through changing circumstances. Any concept is part of a collection of concepts through which the world is perceived. For example, 'logical positivism', sharing many features with 19th century *Utilitarianism*, dominated British philosophy in the 1960s but no longer does so, though it lives on uncritically in the dominance of educational measurement, much like Robert Lowe's 'payment by results' of the Newcastle Commission.

Two concepts I wish to pick out, which are central to one or more of the three traditions outlined above. A grasp of the changing characteristics and thus understandings of those concepts is essential to understanding the evolving debates in education at the foundations of the educational system and continue to do so in planning for the future.

It should be mentioned, however, that in the deliberations of education and in the subsequent policies and practice, the different philosophical positions do themselves inter-relate. One can be both an *Idealist* and a *Socialist*!

Equality

Reference was made earlier to the many struggles amongst working class groups for the enhanced education which would improve their chances in life, would enable them to contribute to the political responsibilities of citizenship following the reforms of the Franchise Acts of 1867 and 1884, and would open up to them the world of ideas and culture – in the words of Thomas Mann, the 'leisure to think, to learn, to acquire knowledge, to enjoy, to develop, in short, leisure to live', namely, what Matthew Arnold would later refer to as the world of culture enjoyed by the upper classes. Such ambitions were encouraged through the many Socialist societies arising throughout the country. For example, it was, as already mentioned, F. D. Maurice who established the Working Men's Club in London in 1854, inspired by his Christian Socialism.

Therefore, there was an increasing criticism of, and indeed hostility to, what was seen as the very unequal society, an inequality in terms of life chances, political influence and quality of life. Such a perception was inevitable, one might think, as educational opportunities were expanded and, one might say, with some influence from the *Idealist* tradition referred to. That 'path' of Plato which led from the dark cave into the sunlight would necessarily have its effect.

However, the key thinker who was to develop an understanding of the glaring inequalities which permeated society and which could not be dealt with without a deeper sociological critique of the class-bound society was R. H. Tawney. Tawney, too, had been a member of Balliol College and much influenced by the *Idealist* spirit, having a vision of what a distinctively human development should consist of. The qualities associated with being 'a gentleman' could be the qualities attained by all through the right kind of education, not to be attainable by the relative few in a distinctive social class and nurtured within the Public Schools of the Clarendon Commission. It was this inequality of aspiration and destiny, associated with the class-based society which Tawney first criticised and attacked. As Richard Titmus, in the Introduction to Tawney's book *Equality* (p. 23), pointed out, Tawney asked the question, 'do the English really prefer to be governed by old Etonians?', and the Appendices to the book provide the data on the kinds of school attended by the leading members of the different and influential professions of the Law, Church, Home and Foreign Civil Services, Banks and Railway Companies. They are overwhelmingly from the very limited number of Public Schools, demonstrating the limiting class structure of society and therefore the extremely limited ladder of opportunity afforded by the education provided at Elementary or indeed Endowed Grammar Schools.

By contrast, Tawney sought a system which emphasised every person's uniqueness and possibility of fulfilment 'without regard to the vulgar irrelevancies of class and income'.

It is the fact that men possess in their common humanity a quality which is worth cultivation, and that a community is most likely to make the most of that quality if it takes into account in planning its economic organisation and social institutions – if it stresses lightly differences of wealth and birth and social position, and establishes on firm foundations institutions which meet common needs and are a source of common enlightenment and common enjoyment.

(Tawney, 1931, p. 15)

Two points should be noted.

First, one sees the *Idealist* influence in the possibility of cultivating in each individual his or her *common humanity* which builds on a *common enlightenment*. Equality between human beings, whether upper or lower class, should lie in their common humanity, but that equality is negated especially by the all-pervasive class system, as reflected in the belief of Thring, the founder of the Headmasters' Conference, in assuaging the apprehension of the rich at the, extension of education, that

'the law of labour' compels the majority of children to work for wages at the age of ten, and it is not possible that a class which is compelled to leave off training at ten years of age can oust, by superior intelligence, a class which is able to spend four years more in acquiring skill.

(Tawney, 1931, p. 33)

Therefore, as stated by Tawney in the Preface (1931, p. 29),

We can certainly, if we please, wind up for good and all the whole odious business of class advantages and class disabilities, which are the characteristics and ruinous vices of our existing social system.

The second point, however, is that such a negation is created or enhanced by the very unequal economic structure through which quality of life is formed, Therefore, that vision of 'common humanity' and 'common enlightenment' is thereby rendered impossible without a 'conversion of economic power'. Indeed, the first chapter of his book, *Equality*, is entitled 'The Religion of Inequality'. Therefore, such an economic analysis takes the '*Idealist* Tawney' into *Socialism*, for, in a socialist community, differences of talent would certainly be recognised in relation to academic achievement and subsequent progress, but such achievement and progress would not be created by contingent economic structures. Therefore, there is a duty for society, first to overcome the unnecessary economic structures which themselves create educational advantages and disadvantages, and, second, to provide the educational framework which responds to young people at different ages and with different capacities and talents – effective ladders for progression. Much of the subsequent sections of the book analyse critically these structures of the capitalist system, indicating the radical reforms required and the educational challenge identified by Arnold when arguing that

> a nation acts unwisely in stressing heavily distinctions based on birth and money. [Rather should there be] the expansion of our humanity, to suit the idea of perfection which culture forms' – though it will take a generation before the benefits of such an expansion can yield their fruit.
>
> (Tawney, 1931, p.226)

It is necessary, therefore, to examine carefully what is meant in this developing debate by 'culture' and, in particular, the key text of Matthew Arnold, much influenced by the Idealist tradition, but now shaping the debate on equality and the future of education.

Culture

The key and most influential text, drawn upon by Tawney, as we saw, was that of Matthew Arnold, son of Dr. Thomas Arnold who was, as noted above, a member of the influential Balliol philosophers who contributed to the National Commissions on the 'Public School'.

Matthew Arnold's *Culture and Anarchy*, first published in 1869, and sub-titled *An Essay in Political and Social Criticism*,

> was to recommend culture as the great help out of our present difficulties; culture being a pursuit of our total perfection by means of getting to know, on all the matters which most concern us, the best which has been thought and said in the world; and through this knowledge, turning a stream of fresh and free thought upon our stock notions and habits, which we now follow staunchly but mechanically.

Arnold was appointed Inspector of Schools in 1851, a post which he held for over thirty years and which required his wide travel around England visiting the Elementary Schools that had been under Government control for twelve years, and thereby giving him insight into the needs of the very poorest of the children, as was noted in Chapter 1. One of his duties was to report on education in the continent of Europe for the Newcastle Commission on Elementary Schools (and later in 1865 to the Taunton Commission). Contrary to Robert Lowe, of the 'Payment by Results' fame, and indeed many of the Commissioners, Arnold defended the capacity of the poor working class to access the insights and the self-knowledge gained through *Culture* which was generally thought to be accessible only to the upper and middle classes through their distinctive forms of education. At the heart of such 'culture' was the 'disinterested' criticism made possible through acquaintance with 'the best that has been thought and said'. Arnold, however, thought that eventually such would be achieved when everyone learnt self-discipline through *Culture* which seeks to do away with classes, thereby

making the best that has been thought and known in the world
everywhere.

Thus, Henry Sidgwick (1867) wrote in his book, *The Prophet of Culture*, (p. 53)

> If any culture really has what Mr. Arnold in his finest mood calls its noblest
> element, the passion for propagating itself, for making itself prevail, then let
> it learn 'to call nothing common or unclean'. It can only propagate itself
> by shedding the light of its sympathy liberally by learning to love common
> people and common things and to feel common interests. Make people
> feel that their own poor life is ever so little beautiful and poetic; then they
> will begin to turn and seek after treasures of beauty and poetry outside and
> above it.

Three observations need to be made in grasping what Arnold meant by culture as
'the best that has been thought and said'. The first is that each person has the capacity to pursue the truth through critical reasoning. The second is for each to develop
a sense, through such critical reasoning, of what sort of life is worth pursuing – the
search for perfection (too often stymied by the way of life assigned to one). The
third is to be able to appreciate the aesthetic dimension to life. Culture therefore
is defined in terms of the pursuit of truth, goodness and beauty through a life of
critical engagement with what, over the generations and over different attempts
to define culture, has been thought, said and created elsewhere. The example *par
excellence* would no doubt be found in Plato's Socrates, whose critical questioning
pursued such goals.

Such critical reasoning should be the basis of community life and decisions,
permeating the political life of the State and, made possible by this broad education
for all, enabling all social classes – indeed, eventually rendering the class divisions in
society irrelevant.

The observation by Sidgwick was most apposite in this regard, for Arnold sought
so to elevate the education of the working class that class divisions would become
irrelevant, that there would be a common educational experience of well-informed
criticism permeating all classes, thereby enabling all to play active parts as citizens
in the expanded political system and all to have the fulfilling lives enjoyed by the
minority.

This, however, leads to an expanded understanding of culture. We have seen
how William Morris, in his book *On Art and Socialism*, in 1884, recalled 'the age of
the craftsman' when pride could be taken in the skill (and in the appreciation and
social contribution) of what he produced – the very aesthetic dimension and social
usefulness which he saw to expand the cultural life which had earlier been defined
by Arnold and which ensured a sense of pride and dignity in what too often was
demeaned. To repeat what was earlier quoted from Sidgwick,

that their own poor life is ever so little beautiful and poetic;
gin to turn and seek after treasures of beauty and poetry
it.

nt

critical in the development of education as there gradually
ll young people, including (as we saw in Chapters 2 and
3) those who would leave school early to enter apprenticeships or the few who
were to progress into higher education. We saw then the embodiment of particular
philosophical understandings of what it means to educate, which understandings
continued to shape the educational system and the experience of the learners into
the 20th century – and (one might argue) still do into the 21st. As was stated in the
Introduction, quoting Gary McCulloch:

> It is hard to understand education without recognising its historical charac-
> teristics… The interplay of past and present has special resonance when we
> are dealing with education. It offers us ample opportunity to make use of the
> wisdom of the past.

There were, as we noted, very different philosophical positions shaping the mindsets of those who were creating the system, particularly those inheriting the
Utilitarianism of Jeremy Bentham and James Mill and those so strongly influenced
by the continental Idealism of Hegel and Fichte. But such was, and is, the strength
of such influences that, in different ways, they continued to underpin so much
educational thinking and planning into the 20th and now 21st centuries. Robert
Lowe's 'payment by results' of the 19th Century lives on in the 'Measurements of
Achievement' of the 21st Century. Examination, criticism and reform of educational practice Proposals should not ignore the ideas which they embody or their
history of the past.

On the other hand, one must be careful not to draw too sharp a contrast
between these different strands in the understanding of the emerging system. The
Socialist ideas of Marx and others strengthened the struggle of those who established secular and even religious societies to liberate the workers from the poverty
and drudgery of their lives, and enabled them to aspire to a share in the world of
'sweetness and light' as defined by the Idealist, Matthew Arnold. R. H. Tawney, a
once member of the Balliol *Idealists*, was inspired by Arnold's definition of 'culture',
yet, in pursuing it as the ideal for all, wrote possibly the most influential critique of
the social inequality and social class which had denied that ideal for the majority
of the community.

Already mention has been made of the special occupations of the labouring
poor, partly inheriting the tradition of medieval apprenticeships. However, the
nature of these – of the kind of knowledge which they required and of the sense of
dignity and satisfaction which they could bring – seemed to play little part in the

philosophical and political debates which took place, until that creative combination of *Idealism* and *Socialism* which is to be found in the work of F. D. Maurice, William Morris and John Ruskin (*developed further in Chapter 3*). They argued for the dignity and sophistication of knowledge and skill in the design and making of physical objects. Unfortunately, such ideals seem to have failed to make a mark in the development of the educational system.

References

Arnold, M., 1869/1963, *Culture and Anarchy: An Essay in Political and Social Criticism*, Cambridge University Press.

Barrell, J., 1830, *Introduction to Coleridge*.

Bentham, J., 1823, *Introduction to the Principles of Morals and Legislation*.

Bryce Commission, 1895.

Bryher, S., 1929, *The Labour and Socialist Movement in Bristol*.

Coleridge, S.T., 1830, *The Constitution of Church and State*, London: Dent and Sons.

Copleston, F., 1966, *A History of Philosophy*, Vol. VIII, London: Burns and Oates.

Gordon, P. and White, J., 1979, *Philosophers as Educational Reformers*, London: RKP.

Maurice, F.D., 1866, *Representation and Education of the People*.

Mill, J.S., 1863a, *Utilitarianism*.

Mill, J.S., 1863b, *Dissertations and Discussions*.

Morris, W., 1884, *On Art and Socialism*, edition, 1947, Holbrook Jackson.

Sidgewick, H. 1867, The Prophet of Culture, MacMillan Magazine, August.

Simon, B., 1965, *Education and the Labour Movement, 1870–1920*, London: Lawrence and Wishart.

Sutherland, G., 1973, *Matthew Arnold on Education*, Harmondsworth: Penguin Books.

Tawney, H., 1922, *Secondary Education for All*, London: Allen and Unwin.

Tawney, H., 1931, *Equality*, (4th edition revised, 1964), London: Allen and Unwin.

11

POSITIVISM, POST-MODERNISM, WISDOM OF THE MARKET

Introduction

In the references to the philosophical understandings which underpinned the changing concept of education and its provision, scarce reference has been made to the underlying political philosophies which have influenced how policy should be formed and political decisions made. And yet there prevail conflicting differences as to how the system of education should be formed, monitored and controlled. The following sections, therefore, make explicit the different underlying philosophical positions which have shaped, and continue to shape, policy in the UK and in the USA.

Dominant strain of 'positivism'

The 'Enlightenment' of the 17th and 18th centuries shaped philosophical thinking for centuries to come, reflected in the empirical tradition in Britain associated with Hobbes, Locke, Berkeley and Hume. According to David Hume (1751) in his *Inquiry Concerning the Principle of Morals*, conclusions drawn from any basis other than purely logical premises, or from what can be sensibly observed and measured (as in science), should be 'committed to the flames for it can contain nothing but sophistry' (*XII, Part III*). The authority of the State lay (as with Hobbes, 1651, in *Leviathan*), in the social contract between citizen and the State to protect the freedom of the individual. Other than such a foundation for a social contract, there could be no objective or rational way for deciding that one form of life is superior to another. Hence, in education, as in everything else, the system would seem to be good or bad in so far as it proves to be socially useful (for example, in providing the skills which the economy needs) or to maximise human happiness amongst the greatest number of people, as reflected in the work of the Utilitarian, Jeremy Bentham, who, in seeking the greatest happiness of the greatest number, provided the first theory of cost-benefit analysis in social and political reform which extended to

> what calculations shall compute the aggregate mass of pleasure that may be brought into existence.
>
> (see Dabhoiwala, 2012, p. 32)

Thus began a tradition within the positivist spirit of social reform through what Anthony Heath (2000) refers to as 'political arithmetic'.

Here we see the 'utilitarian influence', as explained in the first chapter, brought into political decision making by the proposal for 'payment by results', introduced by Robert Lowe in the 19th century, then in charge of the Education Department, and in keeping with the purposes of the Newcastle Commission, as described in Chapter 1. Payment to schools would depend on the tests (what can be measured in relation to specific goals) set by the visiting inspectorate. As Lowe declared to Parliament (Simon, 1960, p. 349),

> I cannot promise the House that this system will be an economical one, and I cannot promise that it will be an efficient one, but I can promise that it will be one or the other. If it is not cheap, it shall be efficient; if it is not efficient it shall be cheap.

It was, therefore, incorporated into the *Revised Code* of 1863.

The underlying belief was that what is real can be observed and measured, explained causally and thus (now with the empirical help of the *social* sciences) changed to meet what are said to be 'improved standards'. These standards can be analysed into what is to be precisely measured. Hence, the importance of so much educational research which endeavours to show empirically 'what works'. This is clearly put by Guba and Lincoln, 1989, p. 12, in their influential book, *Fourth Generation Evaluation*

> The methodology employed [in educational research] has been almost exclusively scientific, grounded *ontologically* in the positivist assumption that there exists an objective reality driven by immutable natural laws, and *epistemologically* in the counterpart assumption of a duality between observer and observed that makes it possible for the observer to stand *outside* the arena of the observed.

Such belief was reflected in the 'language of management' *as exemplified in Chapter 8 of this book*, within what was referred to as the 'modernisation of services' with a view to the 'improvement of standards'. Such a view permeated 'the reform' of public services, including that of education (see White Papers from H.M. Treasury and the Cabinet Office which sought 'public service agreements', for example: in 1988, *Modern Public Services in Britain: investing in Reform*; and in 1999, *The Government's Measures of Success*). What was common to the Government's modernisation programmes was the spelling out of standards in terms of measurable targets which would shape, for example, the curriculum of schools and thus the 'teaching to the test', as so well described in Mansell (2007) *Education by Numbers: the tyranny of testing*. The increasing influence of 'management-speak' was emphasised particularly by the new word 'deliverology'. Schools were increasingly required 'to deliver' higher and measurable standards.

Underlying such a view was, and is, the 'Enlightenment understanding' that there is no way in which one could get at a reality beyond what can be perceived. What are perceived are the sense-data of shapes, colours, sounds *et cetera* – best illustrated by the Scottish Enlightenment philosopher David Hume, and in England by John Locke and Bishop Berkeley. We cannot know what (if anything) exists outside or beyond those perceptions.

Such a philosophical position was articulated by Auguste Comte in *Course in Positivist Philosophy*, and reflected in Britain in the 'logical positivism' of A. J. Ayer. In *Language Truth and Logic*, Ayer argued that only those statements can be verified as true which can be demonstrated as such either by what can be observed and measured or by logic as in mathematics. All other statements are simply meaningless. Thus, for example, so-called moral 'truths' are mere expressions of feelings – the 'emotive theory of ethics' (*see* Ayer, 1936, *Chapter 6*). One might add, too, that attempts to state, or to argue for, the general aims of education must be meaningless also.

It was seen to be important, therefore, in setting the goals of education to identify, first, those goals in terms of specific *targets*, rather than general aims (the extent, therefore, to which they are reached being observable), and, second, the routes by which those targets might be hit (e.g. the appropriate teaching method), demonstrable through empirical research.

Four observations need to be made regarding such an influential philosophical position affecting the development of the educational system.

First, a rational basis for determining *the aims of education* would seem thereby to be removed from public or political discourse. Such aims come to depend on the subjective views or whims of those who happen to exercise power, exemplified in the omission of 'design and technology' from the EBacc system of qualifications (pointed out in Chapter 5) and in the decline in the perceived importance of the Arts in general education.

Second, such a philosophical position undermines the professional judgement of teachers concerning what is worth teaching, as they are confronted with the behavioural objectives on which they are to be assessed, rather than needing to discern the educational needs of pupils at different stages of social and intellectual development. The 'target-setters' take over. They are freed from broader ethical debates about the aims of education which had characterised earlier Commissions on education from the *Newcastle Commission on Elementary Education* in 1861 to the *Robbins Commission on Higher Education* in 1963 (*see Chapter 1*).

Third, such a 'positivist' position is difficult to sustain completely. For example, in legislating for a National Curriculum in 1988, Government necessarily drew upon the tradition of 'liberal education' which identified distinctive areas for the 'cultivation of the intellect', that is, the different 'forms of knowledge or understanding' through which we have come to understand experience, and the failure to introduce which (as Bloom, 1987, influentially claimed) led to the 'closing of the American mind'.

Fourth, however, the *statement* of such a philosophical theory must itself be meaningless because verifiable neither by the principle of logic nor by empirical observation. As stated above, in relation to Hume, conclusions drawn from any basis other than purely logical premises, or from what can be sensibly observed and measured, should be 'committed to the flames for it can contain nothing but sophistry'.

Post-Modernist response

What then came to dominate philosophical thinking in relation to our understanding of education was what might be referred to as the 'Post-Modern embrace', reflecting the many different perspectives through which we evaluate educational practice but without the seeming rational basis for declaring one viewpoint to be more valid than another (feminist, religious, socialist, materialist, ethnic minority, and so on). Such a *Post-Modern* view was much influenced by the likes of Lyotard, reflected in his book in 1984, *The Post-Modern Condition: a report on knowledge*, and legitimated by those who were in a position to define what counts as knowledge. We cannot see 'reality' except through the 'social constructions' which we have inherited or acquired through our social associations. In no way can one step outside that world of ideas (or 'social constructions') to check whether or not they accurately represent a world existing independently of the ideas themselves. The 'sociology of knowledge', influentially promoted by Thomas Kuhn in *The Structure of Scientific Revolutions* (1970) and popularly reflected in Michael Young's *Knowledge and Control* (1972) argued that, since rationality is defined within particular paradigms, there can be no super-paradigm which referees the one which should dictate our understanding of reality. The notion of 'truth', therefore, intrinsic to the Positivist understanding of the Enlightenment, has to be redefined in terms of 'consensus' because there can be no correspondence between a particular conception of reality and the reality itself. Verification or falsification of our stated beliefs no longer makes sense. We have moved thereby to a 'post-truth society', as argued by D'Ancona (2017) and as reflected in the political debates on education, referred to in Chapter 14.

At one level, of course, this is most relevant. What counts as 'true' depends upon the wider consensus within society (or particular groups within the larger society) as to the nature of that which one is talking about. Success and progress within education are shaped by some overall consensus as to what counts as an educated person, and as we have seen from the developing ideas of education as portrayed in this book, there is no universal consensus on such an issue. Educational aims and success (as depicted in the values of the Public schools and Ancient Universities) was not altogether shared within the technical tradition of the late 19th and early 20th centuries. However, the main difficulty with the Postmodern perspective is that there can be ultimately no rational way of resolving this difficulty. If truth is defined within a particular 'paradigm', then that paradigm can itself be seen to be true only within an overarching paradigm which determines which paradigm is to be considered true. On the other hand, although, as we have seen, different philosophical and social beliefs do change and influence the prevailing ideas of education (and its different understandings for different social classes) it is also the case that such views have gradually developed and diminished as a result of philosophical reasoning, experience and research. Even the 'socially constructed knowledge' is open to criticism through rational appraisal, indicating that it is not just a matter of 'social construction'.

On the other hand, it is important to recognise the importance of the insights within the Post-Modern thinking. People of power and influence can and do determine what constitutes good art or architecture or painting, thereby shaping a particular fashion. What constitutes 'good taste' and 'knowledge' often would seem to depend on who are in positions of power (including political power) to define it as such – a focus of the 'sociology of knowledge' which emerged in Britain in the 1960s, influencing theoretical work in educational theory.

Wisdom of the market

Such 'Post-Modernist philosophizing', however, did not prevent the assertion of a contemporary solution to the problem of how the aims of education, broadly conceived, might be formed and translated into objectives, namely, respect for the *Wisdom of the Market* – that is, the imperative to transfer more power to the 'consumers' (namely, the parents and employers) in the absence of philosophically agreed 'aims of education'. Such a shift was anticipated in Sir Keith Joseph's 'voucher scheme' when he was Secretary of State for Education under the premiership of Margaret Thatcher. The political understanding was that by giving vouchers to parents 'to spend' on the school of their choice such 'consumer power' within an 'educational market' would lead to 'improved standards'. Such standards would refer to success in examinations, as determined, say, by a National Curriculum, but also ultimately to improved employment opportunities. To help with such choice, the achievements of the schools would, through national testing and through other indications of success, be made public. Schools which failed in such a 'market' would presumably go out of business as pupils migrated to schools elsewhere.

As Keith Joseph, founder of the influential think-tank *Centre for Policy Studies*, affirmed in 1976:

> The blind, unplanned, uncoordinated wisdom of the market is overwhelmingly superior to the well-researched, rational, systematic, well-meaning, co-operative, science-based, forward-looking, statistically respectable plans of government.
>
> (Joseph, 1976)

Therefore, the role of 'the market' in raising standards in State schools, was strongly advocated by the Centre for Policy Studies, the leading right-wing think-tank, founded by Sir Keith Joseph and Margaret Thatcher in 1974 to develop a new generation of Conservative thinking, built now on promoting enterprise and ownership. Such promotion required a 'privatisation revolution' and entrepreneurship, assisted by a 'shrinking of the state'. With regard to schools, this would be helped, not only by extending parental choice of schools (assisted by schools' greater accountability in providing evidence for such choice), but also by freeing the schools from bureaucratic control. There would be greater autonomy of schools and encouragement of choice by parents, supported by the public evidence arising from the 'national assessment of performance'.

Hence, inspired by the Charter Schools pioneered in the United States, Academies were introduced to England in 2000 by the then Prime Minister, Mr. Blair, and the associated Free Schools in 2010 by the Secretary of State, Michael Gove, thereby liberating schools from the 'control' of their Local Education Authorities which had been established by the 1902 Act. The Centre for Policy Studies launched the book by Suella Braverman, M.P. (1919) *Fight for Free Schools* which urged the Government

> to double-down on the success of Free Schools by speeding up their expansion and by ensuring that they act *as drivers for competition and innovation* within the system (*this author's italics*).

Behind such a policy lay what might be referred to as a 'shrinking of the state', assisted by co-operation between the New Schools Network, established under the Education Secretary in 2010, following visits by his adviser Rachel Wolf and others to New York's Charter Schools (*see* Wilby, 2010).

In this conception of school organisation, shared (through an organisation called the *Atlantic Bridge* – a special partnership promoting limited government and market liberalisation) between the Charter School movement in the USA and the developing conception of school autonomy in the UK, there can be seen a distinctive and challenging view of schooling that deserved closer but critical examination. It was expressed forcefully by Diane Ravitch (2010, p. 217) in her book dramatically entitled *The Death and Life of the Great American High School*

> NCLB (*No Child Left Behind*) introduced a new definition of school reform. In this new era, school reform was characterised as accountability, high-stakes testing, data-driven decision-making, choice, charter schools, privatisation, deregulation, merit pay, and competition between schools. Whatever could not be measured did not count.

Earlier in Ravitch's book is a basic criticism of the Charter School reforms.

> As it elevated the concept of school choice, the Department of Education destroyed the concept of neighbourhood high schools … Neighbourhoods

were once knitted together by a familiar local high school that served all the children of the community, a school with distinctive traditions and teams and history.

(p. 83)

More, therefore, needs to be said about the prominence given to the 'the market' in the philosophical shaping of social and (in particular) educational aims and institutions. In this it is important to turn to the work of the Austrian/British economist and philosopher, F.A. Hayet, whose book *The Road to Serfdom* had a profound impact on the Prime Minister, Margaret Thatcher and no doubt Keith Joseph's advocacy of the 'wisdom of the market'. Hayet's argument was basically that, where politicians try to influence the economy, the ensuing bureaucracy creates loss of freedom and prosperity for both poor and rich. The solution lies in creating the context for individual freedom to choose between different pathways. Markets help create these different pathways. However, the lack of such freedom of choice, which would be enabled by the market economy, leads to totalitarianism. Hence, the urgent need for decentralisation in order to avoid the abuse of Government power. Central planning is less efficient than free capitalism in terms of development and allocation of resources.

It is not difficult to see the application of such philosophy of liberalism in economic theory and practice to wider issues in governance including education. We have seen in Chapter 7 the increasing influence of the politicians both in school organisation and in the details of what is learnt, determined through very specific targets within the new management of schools. We have seen, too, attempts to resist such bureaucratic control by new sponsors and businesses who seek to offer greater choice of education through Academies and Free Schools – 'free choice' exercised in the 'market place'. Indeed, here one might envisage that there may be greater freedom under a capitalist dictatorship, which gave free rein to competing educational businesses and entrepreneurs, than within a Socialist state which centralised educational planning, thereby leading to totalitarianism over content of curriculum and methods of teaching under the influence of a centralised inspectorate.

A place for 'the common good'?

However, as Sacks (2020, p. 1) points out, the stark contrast between 'freedom of the market', on the one hand, and 'centralised control', on the other, omits reference to the crucial importance of a developed social morality – given that such, in the Post-Modern world, can be seen to make sense.

> Societal freedom cannot be sustained by market economics and liberal democratic politics alone. It needs a third element: morality, a concern for the welfare of others, an active commitment to justice and compassion, a willingness to ask not just what is good for me but what is good for all-of-us-together. It is about 'we', not'us'.

Sacks argues, therefore (particularly in the chapter entitled 'Markets without morals'), that the so-called 'wisdom of the market', within which political objectives are formed and pursued, leads to the benefit of all but only where there is a tradition of social concern for, and promotion of, 'the common good'. This he further argues, with many examples, is rendered increasingly difficult from, first, a gradual deterioration of public standards in respect for the truth and for civil debate, and, second, in the increased acceptance of 'greed' as a motivation for business success, exemplified in the disproportionate rewards accrued by business leaders as they pursue private gain from their economic freedom, indifferent to the common good. As Adam Smith, the philosopher of 'market economics' gently put it,

> It is not from the benevolence of the butcher, the brewer, or the baker that we expect our dinner, but from their regard to their own interest.
>
> *(quoted in* Sacks, 2020, p. 97)

Sacks, in response to this tendency to self-serving under the imperative of economic interest, insists that

> morality is what broadens our perspective beyond the self and its desires. It places us in the midst of a collective social order.
>
> (p. 12)

On the other hand, he accepts that such a conception of morality has, with the emphasis on the liberated individual, given way to the pursuit of 'autonomy' with the sole proviso that one does no harm to others. The moral vocabulary, shaping educational aims, has shifted to the emphasis on the 'me' rather than on the 'us' – 'self-expression', 'self-esteem', 'self-realisation'. As Charles Taylor in *Ethics of Authenticity* argues concerning the 'new morality' in a secular age:

> … spread of an outlook that makes self-fulfilment the major value in life and that seems to recognise few external moral demands or serious commitment to others.
>
> (p. 55)

Therefore, there are required strong moral constraints on the 'wisdom of the market', argued by Lord Devlin (1965) in his book *The Enforcement of Morals*

> Society means a community of ideas; without shared ideas on politics, morals, and ethics, no society can exist.
>
> (p. 10)

Consequently, the development of education for all (its very conception and its institutional provision) requires a constant and evolving debate about standards and aims, based on evidence, but within a moral context of 'human flourishing' and 'the common good'. It must be seen as a central concern of ethics – if the articulation of such concerns and of the search for a socially agreed solution are to makes sense. But this, of course, would be difficult, if not impossible, if 'the Positivists' or the 'Post-Modernists' dominate the cultural and political scenes.

References

Ayer, A. J., 1936, *Language, Truth and Logic*, London: Penguin Books.
Bloom, A, 1987, *The Closing of the American Mind*, New York: Simon and Schuster.
Braverman, S., 2019, *Fight for Free Schools*, London: Centre for Policy Studies.
Comte, A., 1864, *Course of Positive Philosophy*, Paris.
Dabhoiwala, F., 2012, *The Origins of Sex*, Oxford University Press.
D'Ancona, M., 2017, *The New War on Truth and How to Fight Back*, London: Ebury Pre.
Devlin, P., 2010, *The Enforcement of Morals*, Oxford University Press.
Dewey, J., 1916, *Democracy and Education*, New York: MacMillan.
Guba, E.G. and Lincoln, V.S., 1989, *Fourth Generation Evaluation*, London: Sage.
Hayek, F.A., 1944, *Road to Serfdom*, London: Routledge.
Heath, A., 2000, 'The political arithmetic tradition in the sociology of education', *Oxford Review of Education*, 26 (3/4).
Hobbes, L., 1651, *Leviathan*.
Hume, D., 1751, *Inquiry Concerning the Principle of Morals*.
Joseph, K., 1976, *Stranded on the Middle Ground*, London: Centre for Policy Studies.
Kuhn, T., 1970, *The Structure of Scientific Revolutions*, Chicago University Press.
Lyotard, 1984, *The Post-Modern Condition: A Report on Knowledge*, Minneapolis: University of Minneapolis Press.
Mansell, 2007, *Education by Numbers: The Tyranny of Testing*, London: Politico.
Ravitch, D., 2010, *The Death and Life of the American High School*, New York: Basic Books.
Sacks, J., 2020, *Morality*, London: Hodder and Stoughton.
Simon, B., 1960. *Studies in the History of Education, 1780–1902*, London: Lawrence and Wishart.
Smith, A., 1776, *The Wealth of Nations*.
Taylor, C., 1991, *The Ethics of Authenticity*, New York: Harvard University Press.
Wilby, P., 2010, 'Free Radical', *Guardian Newspaper*, 16 3.10.
Young, M.F.D., 1972, *Knowledge and Control*, London: Methuen.

12
PRAGMATISM

Introduction

A major, but controversial, contributor to philosophical thinking about education, especially concerning the relation between the learners' thinking and the formal curriculum, was the American philosopher, John Dewey. As stated in the Introduction to this book, Dewey was accused by Sir Keith Joseph (influential Secretary of State for Education under Margaret Thatcher) of being responsible for all the problems in our schools – an accusation repeated to the present author years later by a Minister of Education under the ministerial regime of Michael Gove. Indeed, Dewey was accused in the United States as 'worse than Hitler' for undermining educational standards (Adler, 1953). And the English philosopher, Professor Anthony O'Hear (who had chaired a Government Committee on teacher education) dismissed Dewey as subverting the central aim of education, namely, to initiate students into the cultural richness which had been inherited. He argued that

> it is highly plausible to see the egalitarianism which stems from the writings
> of John Dewey as the proximate cause of our educational decline.
>
> (O'Hear, 1991, p. 26)

Therefore, in looking at the different philosophical influences upon the changing concept of education and the 'educated person', it is impossible to ignore the work and influence of John Dewey either because his published philosophical theories were seen to be responsible for educational decline or because they ought to be taken more seriously than has been the case by his critics in our understanding of educational practice. Therefore, in what follows, this chapter explores some key ideas of Dewey, the distinctive philosophical position of Pragmatism which underpinned those ideas, and the consequences for a better understanding of and justification for educational practices, especially those reported in Chapters 1 and 2.

Key ideas

(i) *The learner's ways of thinking and experiencing*

From the very start of life, the child's mind is being formed by the experiences received, especially through the social interactions which themselves become more varied and complex. In internalising, and adapting to, these experiences, so does the growing person come to understand the world in a particular way. When the children go to school, therefore, they bring with them mindsets through which the new experiences are sieved, including the more formal curriculum, which may or may not connect with the dominant ideas within the pupils' minds, though possibly stuck on, as it were, for purposes of tests and examinations. But too often that formal curriculum makes little impact on how the pupils really think or see the world or interact with others.

To say that is by no means to demean the formal curriculum. Rather does it mean that connections have to be made between what the school has to offer (the educational theories, if you like) and the dominant interests of the child which are re-enforced by the social practices of the world beyond the school. Dewey, there-fore, 'reaches a technical definition of education', namely, a

> reconstruction or reorganisation of experience which adds to the meaning of experience, and which increases ability to direct the course of subsequent experience.
>
> (Dewey, 1916, p.76)

Too often, Dewey argues, there is a rift between what is taught in school and the mindset of the learners, thereby failing to expand the learners' capacity to see and appreciate the world, the society and other people as they might profitably be understood. It is the job of the educator to make connections and thereby to enrich the mode of understanding even in what were frequently conceived as very basic experiences, as was shown in Chapter 2 with the introduction of the aesthetic dimension to the work of the labourers, skilled or otherwise. Indeed, one might argue that Wordsworth's poetry enables one to see nature in a different and more interesting light, and that the tragedies of Shakespeare expand one's conceptions of human nature and practice.

(ii) *Contrast between 'traditional education' and 'learners' interests'.*

In opposing what Dewey referred to as 'traditional education', he received much criticism from such philosophers as Anthony O'Hear (1991, p.5) who (in criticism of Dewey's so-called 'child-centredness') argued that

> Education … is irretrievably authoritarian and paternalistic imparting to a pupil something which he has yet to acquire. The transition is inevitably between unequals.

Or again, Michael Oakeshott, by contrast with central importance given by Dewey to the interactions between the learners' state of experiencing the physical and social worlds, and the formal knowledge accumulated in the curriculum, refers to school as

> 'monastic' in respect of a place set apart where excellence may be heard because the din of worldly laxities and partialities is silenced or abated.
>
> (1972, p. 69)

Therefore, a contrast (sometimes sharp) was being drawn and challenged by Dewey, on the one hand, between 'traditional education' (the initiation into 'the best that has been thought and said', whether or not this arises from the interests and activities of the child) and, on the other hand, greater 'child-centred education', arising from the encouragement to develop knowledge through the pursuit of the child's interests which (it was believed) would open up significant lines of enquiry that transform the child's understanding.

There had, indeed, emerged, under the influence of the more child- or learner-centred education, many examples of 'the project method' (popularised in schools in the post-war years) and of 'activity learning', referred to positively by the Plowden Report, 1967, and thereby accused by Sir Keith Joseph (in conversation with this author) of 'being responsible for all the problems in our schools').

None the less, the significance of the learner's interests and enquiries was much encouraged by W. H. Kilpatrick's 1918 paper entitled *The Project Method*, in which involvement in a well-conceived project or inquiry, preferably in pursuit of the learner's particular interest, motivated the learner and opened up, under guidance from the teacher, ways in which problems of that kind had been systematically conceived and inherited, and would lead to profounder knowledge of the issues. There seemed to be a shift, therefore, from a curriculum based on the traditional subjects (justified by reference to the 'cultivation of the intellect') to a curriculum arising from the interests of the learner, which interests, however, could and should be enhanced by the cultural achievements to which the learners would be appropriately introduced.

Dewey's criticism of education in practice was that there was often a complete severance between the mindset and motivation of the learners, on the one hand, and, on the other, what was presented as the curriculum in schools. Rather was it the case that (as argued in *The Child and the Curriculum, p. 123*)

> The fundamental factors in the educative process are an immature, undeveloped being; and certain social aims, meanings, values incarnate in the matured experience of the adult The educative process is the *due interaction* of these forces. Such a conception of each in relation to the other as facilitates completest and freest interactions is the essence of educational theory.

In this way, the learners' understanding is reconceptualised through contact with the 'matured experience of the adult' (for example, as stated above, through the teachers' insight into a Shakespearian tragedy or their shared appreciation of Wordsworth's poetry), thereby leading to a gradual, better informed and appreciative transformation of how they think and feel.

(iii) *Child-centredness: accusations and defence*

The consequence was that Dewey was seen to be promoting 'child-centred education', an influence (so it was argued) that helped to shape the analysis and recommendations of the 1967 Plowden Report on Primary Schools, and undermining the traditional conception of education as an introduction to the 'best that has been thought and said', no matter how disconnected that seemed from the interests and thinking of the learners.

There were examples, one needs to admit, where Dewey was seen, wrongly, to champion extreme forms of 'child-centredness', where the educational activities were seen to spring from the interest of the learners. The most prominent example was that of the William Tyndale School, where the children, under the banner of progressive and child-centred approaches, were allowed to select their own activities, unrestricted by the teachers, but which was eventually the subject of the very thorough Auld Report in 1976. That Report was one influence in the determination of Government to assert what might be referred to as 'traditional standards' in schools. Thus, the philosopher, Anthony O'Hear (1991, p. 26), dismisses Dewey's emphasis on the importance of experience, let alone the pursuit of the learner's interests, in this dismissive manner.

> In Dewey, we also find sentimental talk of the value of experience of the child, of the intrinsic significance of every growing experience. Classrooms become miniature Swiss cantons in which everything is up for discussion and negotiation by the whole population. The teacher is no more than a provider of 'suggestions', a 'facilitator, in today's jargon.

Indeed, there are examples from Dewey's publications which might seem to encourage such, for example in *School and Society* (p. 103),

> Now the change which is coming into our education is the shifting of the centre of gravity … . In this case the child becomes the sun about which the appliances of education revolve; he is the centre about which they are organised.

However, it would be mistaken to interpret Dewey's recognition of the mindset and interests of the learner as the sole or major determinant of the curriculum. Society has inherited an evolving culture in the different forms of knowledge and understanding, which address what it means to live a distinctively human life and which therefore aims to make such interests and modes of thinking of the learners more intelligible as well as opening up other interests worth pursuing. For Dewey, therefore, the curriculum needed to reconcile these two – the ways of thinking of the learner and the inherited understandings of experience reflected in the different though developing forms of knowledge arising from the 'conversations between the generations of mankind', but too often becoming in what he referred to in the *traditional curriculum*, as

> unduly formal or scholastic notions of education which easily [become] remote and dead – abstract and bookish'.
>
> (2016, p. 4)

(iv) *Importance of 'community'*

Because of the centrality of 'experience' in the growing understanding of children and young people, social interactions also must play a central part – either in stimulating or in curtailing such interactions. It is from the social connections that ideas originate, are shaped or are trounced. Hence, for Dewey those social interactions, where they are established and leave their mark, constitute the 'cultural environment' for each growing person. Such a 'cultural environment' is in part and inevitably the product also of the interaction with the physical environment as that is communicated within a social community – a matter to be returned to in seeing the relevance of Dewey' *pragmatism* to the recognition of the educational value of the practical livelihoods of apprentices as described in Chapter 2. Thus Dewey argues in *Logic: The Theory of Inquiry*:

> Of distinctively human behaviour it may be said that the strictly physical environment is so incorporated in a cultural environment that our interactions with the former, the problems that arise with reference to it, and our way of dealing with these problems are profoundly affected by incorporation of the physical environment in the cultural.
>
> (1938b, p. 42)

The meanings of words, as held by individual people, lie not simply in dictionary definitions but also in the uses and contexts of those words in particular social groupings – for example, the practical tools with which those apprentices, accounted for in Chapter 2, earned, their living, acquired a certain status and perceived a certain meaning and significance in the tools they used.

However, the significance of the social community and of its nurturing lies also in the shaping of community life through democratic arrangements. Thus, as argued in *Democracy and Education* (1916, p. 4),

> Men live in a community in virtue of the things which they have in common. What they must have in common in order to form a community or society are aims, beliefs, aspirations, knowledge – a common understanding – like-mindedness, as the sociologists say.

Such 'common understandings' can develop at different levels of society, and even then, at each level, to a greater or less extent. One purpose of the school, therefore, is to help develop such community well-being through itself creating shared understandings, through finding ways of reconciling differences constructively, through openness to alternative views. To do this, the school has to embrace many of the features of such a community, attending to others' arguments, tolerating differences and fostering respect for others with different and often opposing views to oneself.

Furthermore, as a preparation for life after school, each school would need to embrace the range of social and religious groups within the broader community, so that each pupil would be enabled to outgrow the prejudices of race, religion and social class through the interactions which take place and through the consistent attempt to understand the other positions on matters of social and moral importance within society. Such a preparation for life received concrete manifestation in Dewey's Laboratory School in New York – an example of the Community School, contrasting with there being several schools within the community arising from choice 'within the market'.

Pragmatism

The title *Pragmatism*, therefore, refers to the way in which learning arises through having to address practical and significant problems, and through the interaction between the received (if tentative) understanding of the situation and the need to adjust in the light of further experience. The subsequent solutions to the problem, helped by the attendant teacher (or Master in the case of the apprentice), would gradually give rise to a better theoretical (even if tentative) understanding of the problems and of their practical solutions, but an understanding which would remain tentative and which would be open to correction in the light of further experiences, criticism and conceptual development. There would be integration of both practice and theory, namely, the beliefs which have arisen from pursuit of problems emerging from experience.

For Dewey, and his followers, this was to be contrasted with the acquisition of theory (as in traditional schooling) which has little or no connection with the child's experience – as are the cases where so much learning is imposed by examination and testing systems, having little impact on the student's practical grasp of reality. Pragmatism, therefore, addressed the problem of the relation between thinking and doing, theory and practice, particularly relevant in making sense of the growth of understanding in the formation of apprentices as described in Chapter 2. Therefore, in accordance with his Pragmatist principles, knowledge (or beliefs) grows out of experience where that is approached critically, and where such critical examination is systematically pursued in the light of evidence and in the consideration of challenging and often opposing views. Education therefore requires open and critical communities, in which schools play a crucial part.

In this respect, it is important to understand how such Pragmatism arose from a disillusion with other philosophical positions which, in Dewey's view, underpinned prevailing ideas of education.

First, he challenged the 'dualism' between mind and body which had dominated philosophy following Descartes and which permeated the pervasive and rigid division in education between thinking and doing, between thought and action. The developing practices of the apprentices, for example, had not been lauded as examples of intelligent practice, and for a long time up to the present a clear distinction has been made between the 'academic' and the 'vocational', between the development of 'thinking' and that of successful 'doing'. Such rigid distinctions (as reflected in Chapter 2), as institutionally perpetuated through different sorts of educational or training institution (reflected in Chapters 3 and 4, and maintained in the 'shifting sands of qualifications' portrayed in Chapter 5) would not easily fit within Dewey's theory of meaning.

Second, Dewey (in his paper 'The influence of Darwinism on philosophy' – *see* Capps and Capps, 2005, p. 285) – also expressed a debt to Darwin's evolutionary theories in accordance with which human beings should not be seen as two substances joined together (body and mind). Rather did Dewey see the theory of evolution as having a radical effect on how we should conceptualise the relation between mind and body, thereby overcoming the dualism which, in permeating philosophical theories of knowledge, permeated also our theories of education.

Third, one might note the similarities between Dewey's espousal of evolutionary theories and Karl Popper's argument in his paper, 'Towards an evolutionary theory of knowledge'. which is to be found in a series of essays entitled *All Life is Problem Solving* (1999).

> My starting point is a very simple proposition – indeed, an almost trivial one – the proposition that animals can know something: that they can have knowledge. For example, a dog can know that his master returns home, on working days, at 6 p.m. and the behaviour of the dog may give many indications, clear to his friends, that he expects the return of his master at that time. I shall show that, in spite of its triviality, the proposition that animals can know something completely revolutionises the theory of knowledge as it is widely taught.

The mind, therefore, becomes a sort of repository of successful anticipation of what will happen if … . Such ways of anticipating further experiences, when proved successful, are internalised and give rise to yet further ways of acting. Thus the solutions to problems (always tentative) give rise to new conceptions of how to proceed, which in turn need to be tested out in experience. In this way theories are developed but always open to further development in the light of further experience. The dog's 'knowledge' of his master's return gives rise to doubt when his master fails to turn up!

Therefore, the central concept within the *Pragmatism* of John Dewey, following C. S. Peirce, is that of 'beliefs', not 'knowledge' – beliefs which are built up through the correct anticipation of experiences, the 'meaning' of which lies in the expected consequences of having such beliefs, but which meanings have to change somewhat when such anticipations fail to occur, thereby giving rise to more comprehensive and adapted set of belief. Thus, there is no such thing as knowledge of a reality *as it is*, quite independently of the beliefs we bring to that reality.

Those beliefs, however, will constantly evolve as doubts arise or as they fail to have the predicted impact or effects, and therefore have to be replaced or adapted. Indeed, the growth of science would indicate, on this view, not the acquisition of knowledge as that had traditionally been conceived, but the development of beliefs which are increasingly justified through experiences predicted, and yet which are always open to further development as they fail to continue to predict correctly and therefore demand constant re-conceptualisation of the problems faced. As with all beliefs, there can be no certainties.

Relevance to changing concept of education

The educational relevance of Dewey's critique of traditional theories of knowledge (influenced much by advances in scientific theorising and understanding) is four-fold.

First, it recognises the practical basis for acquiring language from a very early age, and for gaining thereby every-day beliefs.

Second, as explained in Chapter 2, such a practical basis lies in learning how to act in specific social situations and how to use tools at developing levels of sophistication (as in the apprentice's workshops) – hence, the development of practical knowledge of what works and the developing *meaning* of a tool or indeed of 'rubbish'. For example, the vegetable left-overs *mean* something different to the keen gardener in search of compost!

Third, such a *pragmatic* critique lies in the gradual acquisition of a sense of moral worth through living within a community, let us say the family or church community or school, but also, for example, gained by apprentices within their communities of workers and in the apprentices (for example) gaining aesthetic appreciation of their achievements (as argued by Ruskin, 1849, and Morris, 1881, see pp. 24 and 25).

Fourth, however, the relevance of Dewey lies in seeing the understandings of traditional knowledge to be logically related to the inquiries which gave rise to them and thus to their possibly temporary nature, given the consequences of yet further inquiries which are spurred on by the failure to predict further expected consequences.

References

Adler, M., 1953, *Time Magazine*, 59 (17 March) – interview.
Auld Report, 1976, *William Tyndale Junior and Infant Schools Public Enquiry*, London: HMSO.
Capps, J.M. and Capps, D. (eds), 2005, *James and Dewey on Belief and Experience*, Urbana: University of Illinois Press.
Dewey, J., 1902, Pamphlet, The Child and the Curriculum, in Boydston, J.A. (ed.) 2008, *The Collected Works of John Dewey*, Carbondale: Southern Illinois University Press.

Dewey, J., 1910/1915, *School and Society*, reprinted in Garforth, F.W., 1966, *John Dewey selected writings*, London Heinemann.

Dewey, J., 1916, *Democracy and Education*, New York: Free Press.

Dewey, J., 1938a, *Experience and Education*, New York: Kappa Delta Pi.

Dewey, J., 1938b, *Logic: The Theory of Inquiry*, New York: Holt.

Kilpatrick, W. H., 1918, The Project Method, *Teachers College Record*, 19, 319–334.

Morris, W., 1881, 'On Art and Socialism,'(ed. Holbrook Jackson, 1947).

Oakeshott, M., 1972, 'Education: The engagement and its frustration', in Fuller, T., ed., 1989, *Michael Oakeshott on Education*, Yale University Press.

Oakeshott, M., 1975, 'A place of learning', in Fuller, T. ed., 1989, *The Voice of Liberal Learning*, New Haven: Yale University Press.

O'Hear, A.,1991, *Education and Democracy: the posturing of the Left Establishment*, London: Claridge Press.

Plowden Report, 1967, *Children and their Primary Schools*, London: HMSO.

Popper, K., 1999, *All Life is Problem Solving*, London: Routledge.

Ruskin, J., 1849, *The Seven Lamps of Architecture*, London: Routledge.

13

RESPECT FOR TRUTH

Problems of political discourse

Introduction

From the chapters in both Part I and Part II, it might well be concluded that development of 'education for all' (its very conception and its institutional provision) requires constant and evolving deliberation about educational aims and about the standards to be embodied in such aims. Such a debate necessarily takes one into the realm of ethics concerning (as Jonathan Sacks, 2020, argued) the 'common good' – namely, what within the common good promotes human dignity, and thereby a sense of an 'educated person'. But such a debate encounters philosophical problems, if, for example, the philosophical ethos of *Positivism* dominates (reflected in the spirit of *Utilitarianism*), where 'truth' and 'evidence' relate only to what can be empirically verified, and where, therefore, arguments about the common good, human dignity and educational aims would not be open to verification in that way. Furthermore, such a debate similarly encounters philosophical problems under the influence of the *Post-Modernists*, where it is argued that such ethical questions and answers are but *social constructions*, and their resolution depends ultimately, not on objective evidence, but on those with the power to shape opinion and what counts as 'knowledge' through political control or, for instance, through the social media.

Lessons from the past

Such 'a constant and evolving debate' about the aims of education, which would direct educational changes, did, until comparatively recently, precede political decisions over the policy and practice of education. That was made possible by the explicit distancing of education from the political arena. Indeed, as Anthony Crosland said, when Secretary of State for Education, Government should not venture into what he referred to as the secret garden of the curriculum … The nearer one comes to the *profes-sional* content of education, the more indirect the Minister's influence is, and I'm sure this is right.

(quoted in Kogan, 1971, p. 172)

Hence, the Central Advisory Councils for Education, in both England and Wales (independent both in constitution and in membership) had been established by the 1944 Education Act to conduct investigations and to advise Ministers on general education matters, enhancing the practice of the Consultative Committees estab-lished as far back as the 1899 Act. These were non-political in their membership, and chaired by non-politicians. As was mentioned in Chapter 3, when Dr. Marjorie Reeves was invited to be a member of the Central Advisory Council, she was told by the Permanent Secretary that she must be prepared

to die at the first ditch as soon as politicians try to get their hands on education.

(see Reeves, 2011, p. 187)

As an example of that political independence in deliberation about, and prepara-tion of, policy, the Spens Consultative Committee on Secondary Education, which preceded the key 1944 Education Act, had a membership of 20 and met 70 times over a period of five years, in order to deliberate thoroughly the aims of education relevant to all young people throughout their developing lives. These meetings were informed by sub-committees (whose meetings took 50 days altogether), which added to the expertise of the Commission and provided relevant research and evidence. The Commission consisted predominantly of men and women who were immersed in education at different levels and who were able to bring their practical experience and wisdom to the deliberations. In other words, the Commission and its processes of extensive consultation and deliberation were a model for the very educative processes which they sought to implement in schools, free from political control or influence.

Such a practice of long-term deliberation by representative commissions of experts – informed by evidence, by research and by critical contributions from the professions – was continued after the war into the 1960s, as reflected in several significant Reports which addressed problems arising in schools and higher educa-tion. One may mention here in particular Gittins Report *Primary Education in Wales* in 1967; Crowther Report, *15 to 18*, in 1959; Newsom Report, *Half our Future*, in 1963; Robbins Report, *Higher Education*, in 1963; Plowden Report, *Children and their Primary Schools*, in 1967. There were many others, and there followed from them well-informed policies for education at all levels – in no way the product of the whims of the frequently changing Ministers.

Through all this there remained the fundamental importance of, first, 'the culti-vation of the intellect' and 'of aesthetic appreciation', which had been promoted by the *Idealists* within the classical tradition, and, second, the promotion of 'the com-mon good', so much part of the *Socialist* tradition within the changing social and economic context.

Such deliberations would respect, too, the professional knowledge of the teaching profession (as reflected in the Curriculum Study Group and the Schools Council in the 1960s, *referred to in Chapter 8*) and whose practical engagement with pupils from different, often disadvantaged, backgrounds inevitably challenged the generalities of the theorists. The deliberations would seek out relevant information from the extensive research tradition and major reports which had addressed many of the issues arising.

What the thorough and detailed reports of Central Advisory Councils demonstrated (and others referred to) was the vital importance of thorough deliberation following exposure of proposals to widespread criticism, prior to their finishing with specific recommendations.

These deliberations would respect also, though critically, the conclusions of the philosophical traditions which had dominated educational thinking but which were open to criticism when seen as comprehensive accounts of the educational enterprise. The *Positivism*, which dominated so much intellectual approach, could be seen to have its strict limits, necessarily failing to address key questions concerning the aims of education – for example, what counts as an educated person. The exponents of *Wisdom of the Market* failed to address the moral demands of 'the common good', not only the good of those most benefitting from the pursuit of economic rewards.

In all this there was, and is, the need to respect different views, howsoever wrong they may seem, but with encouragement to challenge them in the light of further argument and evidence. Mutual respect amongst people, despite their interpersonal differences, is crucial in the pursuit of a true and defensible account of the situation and in forming policies and practices which not only work but are ethically defensible. One major difficulty in placing too much power into the hands of politicians – such power not arising from, or accountable to, a wider and expert audience – is the transience of their policies and decisions, glaringly apparent in the constant changes of school qualifications described in Chapter 5.

Lessons not learnt

However, by 2010, when the Act of Parliament was passed with its radical changes to the institutional arrangements for schools under the Academies Programme, the tradition of thorough and objective deliberation of the issues (namely, the consequences for the system of education as a whole, or for the underlying philosophical ideas such as the significance of 'the market') was ended. Education, despite the Permanent Secretary's warning to Marjorie Reeves in 1944, had been handed over to the politicians. The tone of educational debate changed as incoming Ministers believed that they had the secret to the achievement of higher standards and educational success, reflected, for example, in frequent changes to the system of qualifications by which 'standards' would be redefined (*see Chapters 5 and 8*) and in the language of management, from within a much more *positivist* perspective which took control as part of the 'modernisation of public services', as explained above and in Chapter 8.

Furthermore, the language of debate and discussion shifted from careful analysis and use of words to emotive language and rhetorical flourishes to produce the required impact upon those to be persuaded. According to the *Prospect Magazine*, a linguistic analysis of the Brexit debate (for example, in the House of Commons, 25 September 2019) showed that the Prime Minister used words from the Harvard University's list of semantically hostile terms every 28 words, roughly every one and half sentences – words like 'traitor', 'betrayal' and 'surrender' in describing his opponents (referred to in Sacks, 2020, pp. 26 and 163, sqq.). And current decisions affecting different educational values and arrangements are similarly lacking in a clear appeal to argument and evidence. Rather is parliamentary debate too often characterised by shouted interruptions and jeers, behaviours which would not be permitted in schools where informed debate in the light of evidence would be encouraged and where support for alternative views would be listened to with respect.

Change in the advisory service

It is worth repeating the advice given to Dr. Reeves when appointed to the Central Advisory Council for Education in 1944, namely,

> Be prepared to die at the first ditch as soon as politicians get their hand on education.

Government departments were served by a Civil Service, within a long-standing tradition of political neutrality, independence of judgment and impartiality, and characterised by core values of integrity, propriety and objectivity in serving the public interest. Recruits were chosen in open competition. They would be familiar with the key reports and evidence relevant to decision to be made, and would advise the Ministers accordingly. They would service, too, the major Commissions referred to.

However, all that changed in the 1960s when there began radical changes in educational policy with development of political control over the management of schools and over the curriculum, including the creation of a National Curriculum and much greater accountability through testing and reform of qualifications. A new order of politically appointed civil servants (not appointed by open competition) called Special Political Advisors (SPADs) was introduced to the different Ministries, including Education, alongside the traditional Civil Service with its distinctively non-political affiliation. All this was part of what was referred to in the 1999 White Paper, as 'Modernising Government'. Mr. Gove, for example, as Secretary of State for Education in 2010 appointed Dominic Cummings to be his special adviser, subsequently to be that of Boris Johnson in the Cabinet Office. It is during this period of office that one witnessed the curbing of the independence of the Civil Service. In his book *Democracy for Sale*, Peter Geoghegan (2020) features several interviews with the American Steve Bannon, key adviser to Donald Trump's election victory in 2019. These interviews reveal a shared interest with Cummings in the reform of the British Civil Service. Bannon advocated demolishing it entirely, arguing administrative state needs to be taken apart brick by brick.

(*Observer, 02.08.20, p. 15*)

Hence, we have witnessed the Head of the Civil Service and Secretary to the Cabinet Office Sir Mark Sedwill, finding it necessary to step down from his post, and also from the role of National Security Adviser, thereby undermining the impartiality of the Civil Service. According to the FDA (First Division Association)

> No. 10 – or those around it – has sought to undermine Sir Mark and the leadership of the Civil Service, with a series of anonymous briefings against him over many months. Not only is it a self-defeating and corrosive tactic, it's also a cowardly one, safe in the knowledge that those who are briefed against are unable publicly to respond.

(Guardian, 29th June 2020)

Two other 'Permanent Secretary victims' have been Sajid David, Chancellor of the Exchequer, and Sir Philip Rutman, Permanent Secretary at the Home Office. As I write, news has come through of the dismissal of Jonathan Slater, Permanent Secretary at the Department of Education, having to resign and give way to one who previously had been private secretary to Prince William.

Post-truth society

The 'ghost' of *Post-Modernism* therefore hangs on, even within (though unself-consciously) the political debates and influence of today, as 'truth', 'evidence' and 'objectivity' do themselves seem to have become ephemeral concepts. Indeed, it is increasingly being seen as a period of 'post-truth', defined by the Oxford English Dictionary in 2016 (as its 'word of the year'), as

> relating to or denoting circumstances in which the objective facts are less influential in shaping public opinions than appeals to emotion and personal belief.

All this is made easier by the way in which ill-formed opinions attain access to the influential social media without the critical engagement which the search for truth would expect. As Sacks (2020, p. 164) quotes

> A lie will go round the world whilst the truth is pulling its boots on.

One might add, too, to the above definition, the false and debasing use of language, as illustrated above, which too often hits the speeches and papers on education where such words as 'standards' (improving or declining) are applied without clarity of meaning or evidence for their use. There is a need, therefore, to think more clearly: first, about the 'concept of truth' (and how to distinguish it from 'fake news'); second, different modes of discourse in which 'truth' is claimed (and thus different modes of verifying what is being claimed to be true in terms of relevant evidence); third, the ideal of 'objectivity', characterising the search for 'truth', in the often controversial debates over education.

First, 'truth' is applied to statements, and it assumes a relationship between such statements and a reality or standards existing independently of the subject making those statements, which reality or standards verify or falsify their correctness. For example, in mathematics and logic truth lies in not offending the principle of contradiction. For the *Positivist*, such verification ultimately depends on a one-to-one relation between the basic elements in the statement and the objects in the world external to the subject. As A. J. Ayer (1936) so cogently argued, the meaning of a statement lies in the mode of its verification. 'This ball is round' is true if it describes something perceived which has that particular feature. The theory of meaning does of course become more complicated than that because there may be several different ways of describing reality (different but perfectly valid 'social constructions' for different purposes), arising from different theoretical perspectives. As Karl Popper (1972) argued in his book *Objective Knowledge: an evolutionary approach*, 'knowledge grows through criticism'. Our prevailing understandings, even based on science, will no doubt be superseded as a result of further experience and scientific work. 'Certainty' always eludes us, and hence claims, which are made, need constant rethinking, but such rethinking is constrained by a reality independent of our conceptions of it. The philosopher Thomas Aquinas put it well: *objective quoad id quod concipitur, non autem quoad modum quo concipitur.*

Second, however, there are different modes of discourse other than empirical and logical claims as to what is the case. There are 'moral claims' as to what ought to be the case, 'aesthetic' as to what is to be valued in the arts, 'religious' as to a divine presence in nature, 'historical' about the past, 'personal' about other's motives. Each kind of claim is within a form of discourse which has evolved over many years through appeal to sensible experience, to personal interactions, to philosophical criticism, to a sense of the spiritual – part of what Michael Oakeshott (1962. p.488) referred to as the 'voices in the conversation of mankind'. Moral argument and judgment, for example, have a history which has evolved through social deliberation, well-articulated in Aristotle's *Nichomachaean Ethics*, but reflectively applied to different ages, circumstances and forms of life. Within each form of discourse, there are standards to which reference explicitly or implicitly is or needs to be made.

Third, therefore, 'objectivity' lies in seeking clarity in the claims being made and in the sort of evidence which justifies them within that form of discourse, including the degree of certainty with which the claims to truth can be held. It is the case that further evidence might arise which challenges the claims being made in each form of discourse, often stimulating philosophical reflection on the nature of the conclusions reached. For example, changed understanding of sexual identity leads to reappraisal of the judgments made within the moral context. Hence, 'objectivity' lies, first, in the search for clarity over what is claimed to be true; second, in review of the evidence on which such claims are being made; third, in the critical examination of the relation of that evidence to the conclusions reached.

Concluding comment

Political pronouncements on education have too often emerged from partisan and uncritical assumptions about the nature and purpose of education, with unquestioned assumptions, too, of overarching philosophical views such as those referred to in previous chapters. One has seen the problems arising from the undermining of clear and objective, evidence-based deliberation, free of political partisanship (which used to prevail) but now proceeding to many of the features of what has been referred to as the 'post-truth society', that is, decisions made without the open, critical and evidence-based deliberation which would lead to an understanding of 'education for all' and of its appropriate provision in a swiftly changing society.

References

Ayer, A.J., 1936, *Language, Truth and Logic*, London: Penguin Books.

Geoghegan, P., 2020, *Democracy for Sale*, London: Head of Zeus, Ltd.

Kogan, M., 1971, *The Government of Education*, London: Macmillan.

Kogan, M., 1987, 'Plowden Twenty Years On', *Oxford Review of Education* 13(1).

Oakeshott, M., 1962, *Rationalism in Politics and Other Essays*, London: Methuen.

Popper, K. 1972, *Objective Knowledge: An evolutionary approach*, Oxford: Clarendon Pres.

Reeves, M., 2011, *Unpublished Memoirs: The Life and Thought of Marjorie Reeves (1905–2003)*, Lampeter: The Edwin Mellen Press.

Sacks, J., 2020, *Morality: Restoring the Common Good in Divided Times*, London: Hodder and Stoughton.

Spens Report, 1938, *Secondary Education: with special reference to Grammar Schools and Technical High Schools*, London: HMSO.

PART III
Conclusion

14

AIMS OF EDUCATION

Human flourishing and development of persons

Introduction

The developing history of education (indeed, the very idea of 'being educated') would seem to have led to an increasingly broader and more inclusive understanding of what counts as 'education' and thus to a wider range of educational provision for all. Such a history reflected not only economic and social developments, but also background (and often conflicting) philosophical understandings of that social reality. Such philosophical understandings are often not explicit. One purpose, therefore, of Part I was to identify very briefly their changing, if implicit, influences on this historical evolution of concept and practice, which were held by different exponents of education and which were intrinsic to the institutions promoting it. The purpose of Part II was to reflect more deeply on those philosophical assumptions, drawing attention to their influences on our understanding of the aims of education but also of their limitations.

It is worth pointing out that the aspiration of 'education for all' would be a considerable advance on Gladstone's claim (*see Chapter 1*) that

> the maintenance of aristocratic exclusiveness [required] a form of education which was remarkably different from that available to other classes.

Therefore, in this concluding chapter, it is important to identify and to summarise this broader and emerging concept of 'education for all' with a view to characterise what, in this day and age, should be seen to constitute an 'educated person' and thus the very aims of education to be pursued for everyone. In so doing, and as revealed in the historical account, the conclusion picks out eight aspects which should be the aims of education.

The emerging aims of education

The emerging aims (clearly interrelated) might be summarised as

(i)   Respecting a common humanity;
(ii)   Extending access to the cultural inheritance;
(iii)   Promoting practical intelligence and competence;
(iv)   Promoting ethical social awareness and deliberation;
(v)   Preparing for citizenship;
(vi)   Preparing for employment;
(vii) Appreciating religious understanding;
(viii) Wider personal development.

(i)   Respecting a common humanity
Throughout these earlier historical accounts, there was a constant plea for respect for the 'common humanity' across social classes and economic functions, most emphatically put by Tawney (1931/64, p.141; see Chapter 3).

> The purpose of the educationist is to aid [*all children's*] growth. It should be easy to regard them, not as employers or workmen, or masters and servants, or rich or poor, but merely as human beings. Here, if anywhere, the spirit of equality might be expected to establish its kingdom. Here, if anywhere, it should be possible to forget the tedious vulgarities of income and social position, in a common affection for the qualities which belong to man himself, and in a common attempt to improve them by cultivation.

Therefore, one witnessed, in these increasing searches for educational reforms, a growing reference to respect for what it means to be, and to become more fully 'human' (now frequently referred to as 'human flourishing') as the ultimate aim of education, affecting all people in 'a common affection for the qualities which belong to man himself'. In the words of Thomas Mann, leader of the Miners' and Dockers' Strikes in the late 19th century (*see Chapter 1*),

> The demand we, as workmen, now make is for leisure, not idleness. Leisure to think, to learn, to acquire knowledge, to enjoy, to develop, in short, leisure to live, we openly and fearlessly declare war against all that tends to keep us riveted to the earth.

However, in so saying, one needs to specify more clearly what those qualities are 'which belong to man himself, to be improved by cultivation', and the attainment of which constitute the aims of education for all, 'irrespective of the tedious vulgarities of income and social position'.

The central importance of such awareness and deliberation as a central aim of education – of being and becoming 'more human' – was clearly put by the Principal of Lawrence Kohlberg's Just Community School, who sent the following letter to newly appointed teachers (*the italics are this author's*), quoted in Strom's 1981 paper, suitably entitled *Facing history and ourselves*.

> Dear Teacher
> I am the survivor of a concentration camp. My eyes saw what no man should witness: Gas chambers built by *learned* engineers
> Children poisoned by *educated* physicians
> Infants killed by *trained* nurses.
> Women and children shot and burned by high school and *college graduates*.
> So, I am suspicious of education.
> *My request is: Help your students become human.*
> Your efforts must never produce *learned* monsters, *skilled* psychopaths, *educated* Eichmans.
> Reading, writing, arithmetic are important but only if they serve to make our children more human.

By way of illustration, two aspects of *common humanity*, emphasised through education in recent years, are those of 'gender equality' and 'equal respect for people of different ethnicity' – recognising all as equally worthy of inclusion in 'the common good' and capable of contributing to it. These aspects surely provide the material for the promotion of *Ethical and Social Awareness and Deliberation* (see Section (iv) below).

(ii) Extending access to the cultural inheritance;

The broader view of education and its provision emerged partly from growing consciousness by the Working Class for 'cultivation of the ordinary soul of the human spirit'. But, as Ruskin, 1853, argued (*see Chapter 2*), 'to brighten, to strengthen, to refine or to reform a single living spirit never enters into our estimate of advantages'. Therefore, it was in pursuit of that 'cultivation of the human spirit', that Thomas Mann 'declared war against all that tends to keep us riveted to the earth'.

The 'spirit of equality', of which Tawney spoke with its implications for an enriched form of education, came to be influenced by the Radical and Socialist Clubs from 1884. Such 'education for all' would raise consciousness, including self-consciousness, through introduction to the culture which had previously been the privilege of the upper social class.

A key 'apostle' of such extension of 'culture' as the basis of education for all, out of respect for a 'common humanity', was (*as explained in Chapter 10*) Matthew Arnold's *Culture and Anarchy: an essay in political and social criticism* (1869). Arnold defined 'culture', which should be the inheritance of all, as

> the general harmonious expression of those gifts of thought and feeling which make the particular dignity, wealth and happiness of human nature'.

Thus, 'culture'

> seeks to do away with classes to make the best which has been thought and known in the world current everywhere; to make all men live in an atmosphere of sweetness and light, where they may use ideas, as it uses them, freely – nourished and not bound by them.
>
> (p.70)

A central aim of education, therefore, in 'serving to make our children more human' (quoting the words of the Principal above) must be to nurture this culture in its different manifestations including the aesthetic dimension of experience. In *Hopes and Fears for the Arts* (1882), William Morris supplied what was missing in *Culture and Anarchy*:

> If art which is now sick is to live and not die, it must in the future be of the people, for the people, by the people; it must understand all and be understood by all.
>
> (Arnold, 1869/1932, Editor's Introduction, p.xxxvi)

Such popularisation of 'culture'. as the basis for education for all, was implicitly critical of the limited understanding of 'culture' which had dominated education provided in Public Schools, where the Classics were seen to

> perfectly express all the principles and mental discipline required to train the statesman, the divine and the gentleman. Critical judgment, taste and facility were held to flow as a natural consequence from a thorough training in Greek and Latin.
>
> (Firth, 1949, p.107)

Such restriction on what counts as 'culture', enforced within the Public Schools and Universities a limited view of what counts as an 'educated person' and provision of different school systems. This broader understanding of 'education', and of those capable of benefiting from it, would need to embrace other disciplines through which knowledge is recognised and intellect cultivated. For example, Phillip Phenix (1964) wrote of different *Realms of Meaning* and Paul Hirst (1974) of different 'forms of knowledge', which should extend the cultural basis of the curriculum, each 'realm' or 'form' characterised by its own distinctive concepts and modes of verification. So, too, as Ruskin (1849 and 1853) and Morris (1884) argued, cultural consciousness would be enhanced through enjoyment of the arts and artistic expression, even to the extent of embellishing working conditions in factories.

Hence, 'cultivation of the intellect' was increasingly seen as initiation into these different form of knowing and appreciating. As Oakeshott (1962, p.488, sq.) explained, experience is revealed in different modes, the 'conversation between the generations of mankind', through which we come to understand the physical, personal and social worlds we inhabit and which can be pitched at different levels of sophistication. Thus education lies in introducing learners to these different modes – the 'voices', for example, of poetry and history, of science and mathematics. Such consciousness would be enhanced by 'acquaintance with enjoyment of the arts and artistic expression'. An aim of education is to move beyond unquestioned common sense judgments about the world, other persons, and values, and to be initiated into the ever deeper grasp and use of these different 'voices'.

As John Dewey explains in his early book, The Child and the Curriculum (1902, p.129)

> Instruction … is a continuous reconstruction, moving from the child's present experience out into that represented by the organised bodies of truth that we call studies.

(iii) Promoting practical intelligence and competence;
This acquaintance, however, with 'the best that has been thought and said' should recognise the intellectual demands and developing traditions of practical work and skills, clearly apparent in the employment and learning of working-class apprentices (*as described in Chapter 2*) but also in the development of technical know-how (*introduced in Chapter 1*) and high-level technology, thereby overcoming the rigid distinction made between 'knowledge that' and 'knowledge how'. As argued strongly in the Spens Report (1938), leading up to the 1944 Education Act (*quoted Chapter 3*)

> We are aware that there are some who would limit the term education to the discipline of faculty and the culture of character by means of the more humane and generous studies, and would deny the name instruction in those practical arts and sciences by means of which man becomes a craftsman or a bread-winner. But this is an impossible limitation as things now stand. We have just seen that the training in classics may have as little liberal culture in it as instruction in a practical art.
>
> (*p. 58*)

Thus, Matthew Crawford, in setting forth the theme of his argument in *The Case for Working with Your Hands* (*Chapter 2, p.22*) emphasised that

> The disappearance of tools [and manual competence, *p.2*] from our common education is the first step towards a wider ignorance of the world of artefacts we inhabit. …… I quickly realised that there was more thinking going on in the bike shop than in my previous job at the think tank.
>
> (*Chapter 2, p.22*)

Richard Sennett (2008) in *The Craftsman* (*also referred to in Chapter 4*), criticised the demeaning of 'intelligent practice', thereby drawing

> fault lines dividing theory and practice, technique and expression, craftsman and artist, maker and user … But the past life of craft and craftsmen also suggests ways of using tools, organising bodily movements, thinking about materials which remain alternative, viable proposals about how to conduct life with skill.

The craftsman and those engaged in practical problem-solving (as results from the teaching of Design and Technology) come to understand matters more intelligently in the context of making or doing, and become able thereby to reflect on that understanding, as they become more practically able to engage in improving their practice. The long tradition of vocational education in Further Education Colleges and Polytechnics (*referred to in Chapter 4*) was based successfully, at different levels, on integrating practical work with greater intellectual insight into what was manually engaged with.

Formal education has a central role in ensuring development of such intelligence through practical engagement as much as it does through initiation into formally organised bodies of knowledge as traditionally conceived. Indeed, the *Pragmatism* of John Dewey (*see Chapter 12*) was critical of this separation of thinking from doing, of theory from practice, which created rigid social distinctions between children and thereby between future citizens. Therefore, Dewey proposed a radically different understanding of the educated person, exemplified in the curriculum of his renowned Laboratory School in New York. In such a school, educational growth comes from taking practical interests of pupils seriously, helping them to deepen their understanding which would include not only the theoretical dimension but also the social and ethical context.

The failure in this matter has created in many Comprehensive Schools a division between the curriculum of the 'academically streamed' and one more focused on craft and practical studies, resulting in the removal of 'Design and Technology' from the list of English Baccalauriate (EBacc) subjects, as explained in Chapter 5.

(iv) *Promoting ethical social awareness and deliberation*
A significant aspect of 'the best that has been thought and said' (in challenging 'our stock notions and habits') would be the ethical awareness which encourages and enables evaluation of one's personal life and social context – questioning values which one is to pursue and which are frequently held unconsciously or without critical reflection. One would be stimulated to do so in the light of what has been eternalised in literature, art, history and social criticism, and (within the inherited tradition of some schools) in religious and spiritual reflection.

Throughout the historical development given in Part 1, one witnessed appeal to moral principles arising from recognition of a 'common humanity' and occasional reference to 'the common good' (for example, Jonathan Sack's account, Chapter 11). Such awareness, however, needs to be enhanced through encouragement of organised classroom deliberation on what is a worthwhile form of life or what are the qualities to be fostered, as illustrated on following pages. Such questioning and deliberation should take place through study of literature, drama, critical examination of success and tragedy explored in history.

However, 'moral deliberation' is shaped also by virtues, and it would be an important aim of education to help form those virtues, particularly of fairness and justice central to 'the common good' and thus to the education in citizenship. But research by Kohlberg (1971) of Harvard University on the concept of fairness indicated that no amount of telling about fairness results in students acting fairly. That led him to create the 'Just Community School'. Values were taught through embodiment in the very structure and relationships operating in the school – inspiring the letter of the Principal of the High School in Cambridge Massachusetts, quoted in *Section (i)* above. Similarly, Nel Noddings, in *The Challenge to Care in Schools*, argues for 'caring for others' and for maintenance of the wider community as a central human value. An essential aspect of becoming a person is to recognise others as persons, with their own distinctive needs, values and capacities for understanding, thereby deserving respect. Such caring for others as persons, living within community, inevitably raises questions about the 'common good'. As Nodding says, 'when I really care, I hear, see or feel what the other tries to convey'. Personal relationship and respect are moral achievements to be fostered through educational experiences – for example, readiness to listen to others' views, and openness to criticism.

It is helpful, therefore, to relate an example of a primary school, which puts pursuit of the virtue of caring at the centre of its educational programme. The school served a very disadvantaged area (of the class of 30, eleven were on the social services 'at risk register'). But the class had learnt 'the rules' for engaging in open discussion of problems which they encountered in their lives – only one person at a time, nothing hurtful of another in the group, everyone to listen carefully to what each said. Interpersonal support was encouraged. But, further, such principles entered into whole school policy, including associations of staff and relations with parents who had their own coffee area within the school. As in the case of Kohlberg's promotion of the virtue of justice, so with 'caring' and the promotion of 'the common good', moral education took place by being embedded (and explicitly so) in classroom and whole school relationships.

(v) *Preparation for citizenship*

As was plain from Chapter 1's account of the Clarendon Commission on the Public Schools, education for citizenship always had a place in the aims of education, but a place limited to the privileged minority who would become (as with Plato's 'Guardian Class') the 'clerisy', so educated through the wisdom of the classical literature and history of the Ancient Greeks and Romans as to acquire 'all the principles and mental discipline required to train the statesman'. Thus the Clarendon Commission created an efficient but segregated system of education for the governing class, and the very limited number of people (all men) who had the franchise and could be regarded as 'citizens'

As the radical reforms of 1870 approached, there was emerging a more positive understanding of education for the working class. As pointed out in Chapter 1, F. D. Maurice (1866), in *Representation and Education of the People*, articulated the beliefs of the London's Working Men's College when he argued that no so-called education would be good for the workers

> which did not recognise them as English citizens and did not aim directly at the object of qualifying them to perform their duties as citizens (*see Chapter 1*).

Thus. 'citizenship' had entered the list of educational aims as a result of antici-pated political reforms. It came to prominence in the Spens Report, 1938 (*see Chapter 3*), leading to the 1944 Education Act. That broader view of the aims of education arose from the struggle (via five Electoral Reform Acts) for political par-ticipation of everyone as citizens (including women – but only from 1902), thereby requiring wider political and social awareness. As Spens Report argued, importance needed to be attached to the development of 'citizenship' through both curriculum and ethos of the school. But such 'citizenship' was conceived more broadly than simply the right to vote. It required development of social conscience, concern for the 'common good', and understanding of the mechanisms which achieved social improvement. This was a key aspect of education to be developed through the cur-riculum and the ethos of the school,

> emphasising the serious character of the social and other problems which have to be faced, and at the same time insisting that, whilst there is need for enthusiasm in causes which are felt to be vital, there is need also for study or judgment.

It is interesting to note the ways in which some schools seek to promote such consciousness. James Honeybone (2020) pioneered *In-Class Debating*, in which the pupils learn to discuss matters of social and personal importance. They are 'taught to listen to the views of their peers and state their views without problems of contra-diction, peer approval or even ridicule'.

> Progressively through his long career Jim taught his pupils to consider issues both trivial and serious, in a way that brings them into the wider society for which they are being prepared and got them there in an atmosphere of open-ness, respect for facts and respect for the views of others.
>
> *(Peter Clifton for 3Score Publishing)*

Such class debates on current but controversial issues took place fortnightly, sup-ported by 'Class Debate Sheets' which clarified terms, identified key issues, and stated controversial claims often by well-known people. Such 'class sheets' or topics included, for example (depending on their public significance at the time), 'LGBT claims', a 'Pro-hunting march through London', 'Parents to be barred from hitting children'.

Learning how to present arguments on controversial issues of wider social sig-nificance and to discuss them on the basis of argument and evidence would seem essential to the maintenance of a democratic society – even more so today as we move politically into what is referred to as a 'post-truth society', recently defined by the Oxford English Dictionary as

> relating to or denoting circumstances in which the objective facts are less influ-ential in shaping public opinions than appeals to emotion and personal belief.

(vi) *Preparation for employment*

Human welfare depends on general economic well-being and therefore on continual preparation of a skilled and literate workforce, especially (*as pointed out in Chapter 2*) with the growing Industrial Revolution requiring workers with technical skills and knowledge. Hence, these needed to be provided and enhanced by a continually reformed educational system, reflected, first, in the apprenticeship system of the 19th century which served economic needs of the time and required workers with particular skills, guided by 'the master craftsman'. But as the economy changed, so there was need for different sorts of preparation – 'the head-worker', as well as the 'hand-worker' – stimulated by the advances in technical education of other countries (as reflected in the Paris Exhibition of 1867) and leading to the Royal Commission on Technical Instruction 1881 to 1884.

Such broader vision of education was captured in the Royal Society of Arts Declaration of Capability (RSA, 1980), recited in Chapter 5.

> There exists in its own right a culture which is concerned with doing and making and organising and the creative arts. This culture emphasises the day to day management of affairs, the formulation and solution of problems, and the design, manufacture and marketing of goods and services.

That 'preparation for employment' was not lost on the changing University sector. The Civic Universities, established towards the end of the 19th century (*see Chapter 6*), were linked closely with regional industrial needs, serving them with relevant scientific and technological research and with broadly educated personnel. And the growth of Further Education, as described in Chapter 4, was a further example of the response to employers' needs.

(vii) *Appreciating religious understanding.*

Many will find it odd that, within an increasingly secular society, understanding and appreciation of religious life should be seen as an aim of education. How can that be if one does not believe? The response must be, however, that (believing or not) understanding and appreciating experience from a religious perspective must be seen as a distinctive element in what it has meant to be human, and thus in the aims of education. One need not be a 'believer' to be moved by and appreciate religious and spiritual perspectives on our understanding of experience in its different modes as expressed in literature, ways of life, music, liturgy or poetry, as, for example, in William Wordsworth's *Tintern Abbey*,

> a presence that disturbs me with the sense of elevated thoughts; a sense sublime of something far more deeply inter-fused whose dwelling is the light of setting suns.

or John Ruskin, quoted in Otto's The Idea of the Holy (1923/1958, p.125)

> Lastly, although there was no definite religious sentiment mingled with it, there was continual perception of Sanctity in the whole of nature, from the slightest thing to the vastest; an instinctive awe, mixed with delight; an indefinable thrill, such as we imagine to indicate the presence of a disembodied spirit.

Education should include appreciation of (even where not committed to) a spiritual dimension to living, enshrined within religious cultures which have been addressed by philosophers from the Greeks onwards and which are captured in the religious traditions that have characterised the world's civilisations. Increasingly is this the case when young people are surrounded by, and initiated into, a distinctively secular understanding of the world. Part of 'human flourishing' would require an understanding and appreciation of an alternative point of view – one which has played so important a part in the growth of our civilisation.

(viii) *On being a person*

It is ironic that A. J. Ayer (whose influential *positivist* concept of meaning and truth was referred to in previous and former chapters) succeeded John Macmurray as Grote Professor of Logic at University College London. Whereas Ayer and 'logical positivists' transformed the language of values to what is measurable (the influence of which is reflected, as explained in Chapters 8 and 10, in the reduction of educational aims to measurable targets), Macmurray (1961, p.12), far from reducing everything to what is a construction from the observable and measurable, wrote of the *form of the personal*. To be a person, and thus to grow and develop as a person, brings to the fore quite different understandings from those which describe purely physical things, which are comprehended within the language of measurement and targets, and which now shape much so-called educational thinking, reducing it to 'inputs and outputs', 'performance indicators', 'delivery' and 'audits' – as explained in Chapter 8 in the section on 'The Language of Management'.

However, can being and growing as a person be so described?

John Macmurray in his Gifford Lectures, 1961, argued for the distinctive 'form of the personal' - the appreciation of what it means to be and to develop as 'a person', thereby the condition for understanding and respecting each other, too often ignored, with particular reference to what could be meant by educating *young persons*. Macmurray's criticism was that, in not recognising their distinctive character as 'persons' (which characteristic needs to be developed), we are in danger of treating children and young people as 'objects' to be used for others' purposes or to be seen as failures, indeed even uneducable within the prevailing systems of education. A broader understanding would recognise each person (including the young child) as having a distinctive consciousness of the world, emotions, values and the beginnings of rationality. All these need to be developed, including the ability to form and examine intended behaviour in the light of what is possible and desirable. The danger, in not recognising the 'form of the personal', is the failure to see in each person (howsoever limited in age and capacity) the possibility of critical awareness of his or her situation and of engaging with moral choices and social realities.

Macmurray's 'form of the personal' defies such a restrictive understanding of development as a person. Persons live in relationships with others and within communities. There are therefore aspects of being a person (not simply academic) which others within the school community should learn to respect, irrespective of academic success. Those aspects include distinctive experiences, backgrounds and relationships which shape how they see themselves and others. From such different experiences are to be developed sensitive relationships, thoughtful acquisition of distinctively human values and moral outlooks, sense of personal achievement and success, and self-respect arising from achievements of different kinds. One sees in schools' attempts through various activities – athletic, sporting, musical, charitable, community engagement – to nurture that sense of personal achievement and self-worth which prepare pupils to contribute positively and with confidence to the wider community they will one day enter.

The question is, therefore, how far the school might, in different ways, nurture that sense of self-respect as well as respect for each other, irrespective of academic achievement. Too often, because of prevailing definitions of failure, only limited aspects of personal development are recognised. Other personal qualities go unrecognised. What is necessary is a broader sense of education which respects development as persons, and in which (back to the opening section of this chapter) their humanity and self-respect are enabled to flourish.

However, mention should be made of this wider understanding of 'personal development' (*as given in Chapter 4*) in the Further Education's support for the Youth Service's work with often the most disadvantaged. As was relayed with regard to some of the least advantaged young people,

> to develop their understanding of themselves, of the alternative possibilities open to them and of a positive way out of the self-destructive form of life, would be a necessary initial stage in an *educational* process, guided by a mentor who could see the possible routes into a healthier form of life.

Human flourishing as the aim of education?

Development of young people in these different ways is often referred to as 'human flourishing' – bringing about the qualities which are characteristic of a distinctively human form of life. One hears speak of plants and flowers 'flourishing', suggesting that such plants and flowers have a nature which, under right conditions, would lead to growth in a distinctive and predictable way. The 'flourishing' would be an expression of their nature. Of course, often the conditions are not right and such growth is stymied – the tomatoes catch the blight and the flowers fail to display their potential beauty. They fail to flourish.

But can the same concept be applied to human beings, such that it makes sense? There seem to be many ways in which humans might develop, and it is not so easy to agree on which is the appropriate outcome (as is the case with tomatoes or flowers). There would seem to be, for example, a difference between a deeply religious person and a committed secularist on what would count as 'human flourishing' – their lives would reflect different goals and values. The reason for this is that humans, unlike plants, have a consciousness as to the ends or goals to which they would like to direct their future growth. They have motives and values which direct their actions and thus future formation. The idea of 'human flourishing', therefore, cannot avoid the ethical questions as to what is a worthwhile form of life – what are the appropriate motives and values concerning the kind of human being they would wish, or ought, to become. What counts for them as *human* flourishing? A significant aspect, therefore, of the educational experience should lie in the assistance in addressing such an ethical agenda. Moral understanding and development would surely be at the centre of the educational enterprise, as argued in the subsection (iv) above.

Much has been written regarding 'human flourishing' as the 'aim of education', fruitfully summarised by Kristjan Kristjanson (2020): *Flourishing as the Aim of Education: a Neo-Aristotelian view*. Although, as he points out, there is the temptation to emphasise the subjective state of mind (of, for example, the contented or 'well-balanced' person, who is able to survive the vicissitudes of life), there would none-the-less be restraints on what can or should be attained, objectively speaking, due to one's distinctive nature as a human being, capable of reflection, with a sense of purpose in life, and within moral constraints which are not simply a matter of personal choice. Such constraints would include espousing and exercising certain virtues which constitute the distinctively human life worth living and which therefore apply to all as well as to the community in which each human being lives and grows. The virtues of justice, patience, courage, perseverance constitute the good life whatever the circumstances one finds oneself in. In practising such virtues, as one strives in one's given circumstances to attain a life which is seen to be objectively worth-while, so one is coming to live a distinctively human life. In so saying, one is claiming a moral dimension to human flourishing which needs to be nourished, including deliberations over the ends which one should pursue.

Conclusion

The eight areas would seem to summarise the key elements in the educational contribution to human development. Such contributions are not confined to academic success but they do emphasise access to the inherited culture, in its different forms, shedding critical light on the struggles, values and possibilities of human life – on what it means to be human and to become more so.

For this reason, one can see the passionate objections, raised in the earlier chapters of this book, to the belief that certain classes of people are uneducable or are unable to benefit from the culture which Chapter has been inherited.

References

Arnold, M., 1869/1932, *Culture and Anarchy*, Cambridge University Press.

Ayer, A.J., 1936, *Language*, Truth and Logic, London: Penguin Books.

Clifton, P., 2020, *Introduction to Honeybone*, 2020, Charbury: 3Score Publishing.

Crawford, M., 2009, *The Case for Working with Your Hands*, London: Viking (The Penguin Group).

Dewey, J., 1902, The Child and the Curriculum, in Garforth, F.W., 1966, *John Dewey: Selected Writings*, London: Heinemann.

Dewey, J., 1916, *Democracy and Education*, New York: Free Press.

Firth, J. D'E., 1949, *Westminster College*, London: Winchester Publications Ltd.

Hirst, P., 1974, 'Realms of Meaning and Forms of Knowledge', in Hirst, P. *Knowledge and the Curriculum*, London: Routledge and Kegan Paul.

Honeybone, J., 2020, *In-Class Debating*, Charlbury: 3Score Publishing.

Kohlberg, L., 1971, *Essays in Moral Development: the philosophy of moral development*, San. Francisco: Harper and Row.

Kristjansonn, K., 2020, *Flourishing as the Aim of Education: a neo-Aristotelian view*, London: Routledge.

Macmurray, J., 1961, *Persons in Relation*, London: Faber and Faber.

Maurice, F.D., 1866, *Representation and Education of the People*.

Morris, W., 1884, 'A factory as it might be', *Justice*, vol. 1.no.18.

Noddings, N., 1992, *The Challenge to Care in Schools: an alternative approach to education*, New York: Teachers College Press.

Oakeshott, M., 1962, *Rationalism in Politic and other Essays*, Liberty Fund Inc.

Otto, R., 1923/1958, *The Idea of the Holy*, Oxford University Press.

Phenix, Realms of Meaning RSA, 1980, *Declaration of Capability*, London: Royal Society of the Arts.

Ruskin, J., 1849/1901, *The Seven Lamps of Architecture*, London: Routledge.

Ruskin, J., 1853, *The Stones of Venice*, New York: De Capo (2003).

Sacks, J., 2020, *Morality: Restoring the Common Good in Divided Times*, London: Hodder and Stoughton.

Sennett, R., 2008, *The Craftman*, London: Penguin.

Spens Report, 1938, *Report of the Consultative Committee on Secondary Education*, London: Board of Education.

Strom, M.S., 1981, 'Facing history and ourselves: integrating a holocaust unit into the curriculum, in *Moral Education Forum (Summer)*.

Tawney, R.H. 1922, *Secondary Education for All* (revised edition 1938).

Tawney, R. H., 1931/64, *Equality (revised edition)*, London: George Allen and Unwin.

NAME INDEX

SUBJECT INDEX

SUBJECTS

Printed in Great Britain
by Amazon

49116508R00104